T0151158

Buddhism in Ten

Ten Easy
Lessons Series

Buddhism in Ten

C. Alexander Simpkins, Ph.D.

&

Annellen M. Simpkins, Ph.D.

TUTTLE PUBLISHING
Tokyo • Rutland, Vermont • Singapore

First published in the United States in 2003 by Tuttle Publishing, an imprint of Periplus Editions (HK) Ltd., with editorial offices at 364 Innovation Drive, North Clarendon, VT 05759-9436 U.S.A.

Library of Congress Cataloging-in-Publication Data

Simpkins, C. Alexander.
    Buddhism in ten / by C. Alexander Simpkins & Annellen M. Simpkins
        p. cm. — (Ten easy lessons series; 3)
    Includes bibliographic references.
    ISBN: 0–8048-3452-0 (pbk.)
        1. Religious Life—Zen Buddhism. 2. Zen Buddhism—Doctrines. I. Simpkins, Annellen M. II. Title. III. Series.

    BQ4302 .S52 2003
    294.3' 444—dc21   2003054044

Distributed by

North America, Latin America, and Europe
Tuttle Publishing
364 Innovation Drive
North Clarendon, VT 05759-9436 U.S.A.
Tel: 1 (802) 773-8930
Fax: 1 (802) 773-6993
info@tuttlepublishing.com
www.tuttlepublishing.com

Asia Pacific
Berkeley Books Pte. Ltd.
61 Tai Seng Avenue #02-12
Singapore 534167
Tel: (65) 6280-1330
Fax: (65) 6280-6290
inquiries@periplus.com.sg
www.periplus.com

Japan
Tuttle Publishing
Yaekari Building, 3rd Floor
5-4-12 Osaki, Shinagawa-ku
Tokyo 141 0032
Tel: (81) 3 5437-0171
Fax: (81) 3 5437-0755
tuttle-sales@gol.com

12 11 10 09   00 9 8 7 6 5 4 3 2

Cover design by Kathryn Sky-Peck
Design by Dutton & Sherman Design
Printed in Singapore

To:
Our parents, Carmen and Nat Simpkins
and Naomi and Herb Minkin,

And to our children, Alex Jr., Alura, and Anthony.

And to Bodhisattvas, whose unwavering compassion
for others continues unceasingly.

Contents

Preface

Buddhism teaches wisdom and compassion. It encourages an inner journey of discovery that helps people find happiness and fulfillment in even the smallest moment. With this deeper awareness, everyday life takes on new meaning—you need not look elsewhere for deep satisfaction. When you open your mind in the right way, enlightenment is possible in the life you live now.

About This Book

In ten lessons, this book presents the important teachings of Buddhism—along with exercises for experiencing, understanding, and applying Buddhism in your daily life. We begin by introducing Buddhism with a short historical overview to give you context for your path ahead. The early lessons contain fundamentals of Buddhism such as sutras, the Four Noble Truths, and the Eightfold Path, with separate lessons devoted to Right Mindfulness, the seventh step, and Right Meditation, the eighth step. Emptiness and Mind-Only are explained and illustrated with exercises to help you make these central Buddhist themes your own. The last three lessons show you ways to apply Buddhism to many areas of life, including enhancing creativity, overcoming obstacles, and discovering enlightenment.

How to Use This Book

Throughout this book, we've suggested exercises designed to help you enhance your skills. Buddhism is best learned by experiencing it for yourself, so we encourage you to try the exercises, enjoy them, and learn from them. You will undoubtedly adapt them to fit your personal journey as you continue to deepen your understanding and broaden your capacities. Nothing holds you back from the unlimited potential of your mind!

Buddhism is an inner experience that is lived in every moment. We encourage you to take these skills and use them in all kinds of ways—solve problems, improve your relationships, and find more fulfillment in everything you do.

Introduction

Historical Background
of Buddhism

All history is the history of thought.
—Collingwood 1957, 215

Buddhism is an ancient philosophy that evolved over the centuries into a world religion. The story of Buddhism formally began with the enlightenment of one man, Siddhartha Gautama (563–483 B.C.). At the moment of his inner transformation he became known as the Buddha, the Awakened One. But the roots of these extraordinary events reach beyond the single man.

Siddhartha grew up in a time when India did not have one central government but consisted of many small kingdoms with separate rulers. His father was the *raja* of one such small kingdom. India was not only decentralized politically, it was also divided intellectually and spiritually. Many different philosophical and religious theories coexisted and vied for acceptance. There were no universally recognized methods for determining

Buddha-to-be-Sakyamuni, artist unknown. Late tenth century, Pala Period, India. Granite. Gift of Asian Arts Committee, San Diego Museum of Art.

Buddhism in Ten

facts. Many religious beliefs and practices flourished. Different groups argued about such topics as the nature of reality and the self, distinctions between truth and appearance, determinism or free will, and the existence of God. The diversity of viewpoints had deleterious effects: Relativity in thought was leading to relativity in morality (Radhakrishnan 1977, 358).

Siddhartha was educated in the differing philosophies and religions and felt the chaotic effects of all the conflicting metaphysical speculation. This setting helped to influence his original formulations for a unified theory based on a definite method for arriving at truth.

The Life of Buddha

Siddhartha was born into his privileged life as the son of the raja of a small kingdom in northern India. But even though he had a luxurious lifestyle, he felt like something deeper was missing. He observed how all people, no matter how privileged, suffered from sickness, old age, and death. So at the age of twenty-nine, he left his beautiful wife and child to seek spiritual answers. He lived a life of self-denial out in the woods with other seekers, meditating on the problems of humanity. But as he neared death from deprivation, he realized that he was no closer to solving the problem of human suffering. He ate a nourishing meal to revitalize himself. Then he vowed not to stop meditating until he found an answer. He meditated under a bodhi tree all through the night. As the sun rose on the new day, he had a profound realization and became the Buddha. He devoted the rest of his life to teaching his system.

Buddha found that a middle way between extremes was the right path to follow. He recognized that too many philosophical theories took people away from the certainty that could be found within. He developed a clear method to discover truth that he called the Four Noble Truths. By following Buddha's procedure, people could come to their own enlightenment. Some scholars have likened his method to an early type of scientific inquiry, since it showed people how to examine their experience in a systematic manner.

Buddha gathered many disciples over his lifetime. Even his father, wife, and son became members of his Buddhist community. He devoted his entire life to encouraging people to seek enlightenment. Some of Buddha's last words reflected his lifelong message: "Be a lamp unto yourself. . . . Work out your salvation with diligence!"

Buddhism Evolves

Following Buddha's death, his disciples gathered together in what was called the First Buddhist Council (483 B.C.). The entire council recited all Buddha's teachings together, committing them to memory. In those days people memorized anything they thought was important to save. The written word was thought to be inferior to the human memory. The disciples went their separate ways, preaching the ideas of Buddha where they traveled.

For the next hundred years Buddhism was passed along orally through direct teachings. Inevitably, differences gradually found their way into the sermons. A second council convened in 383 B.C. to resolve the discrepancies between the traditional versus a newer, more liberal interpretation. The traditionalists won out, and Buddhism became known as Buddhism of the Elders, or *Theravada*.

The Theravadins strove to lead a pure, meditative life, aware and awake in every moment. These monks secluded themselves in Buddhist communities, where they could pursue the pure, meditative life of an *arhat*. There they could stay aloof from the pleasures of daily life and remain committed to finding Nirvana.

The Theravadins held a third council in 237 B.C. where they finally wrote down the teachings. They gathered them into three large bodies of literature consisting of sutras, rules, and commentaries known as the *Tripitaka, The Law Treasure of Buddhism*. Theravada Buddhism spread around Northern India, Mongolia, Sri Lanka, and Southeast Asia, where it continues to flourish in modified form today.

A New Form of Buddhism Emerges: Mahayana

The more liberal contingent also continued to grow, forming an ever-widening rift with the Theravadins. The moderate Buddhists began to gather their own separate doctrines. An entirely new literature evolved between 100 B.C. and A.D. 200. Eventually, the differences between the liberal monks and the Theravadins became so great that the two groups split. The new order called themselves *Mahayana* (Greater Vehicle) and relegated to the Theravadins the name *Hinayana* (Lesser Vehicle). Mahayana spread in Southern India and then to China, Korea, Japan, and Tibet.

Doctrinal Changes from Hinayana to Mahayana

Several clear differences distinguished the Mahayana from the more traditional Buddhism. Today many of the distinctions still exist, although boundaries are more blurred.

The Mahayana developed a new lifestyle for their followers called the *bodhisattva*. Unlike the arhat, who withdrew from society to find Nirvana, the bodhisattva lived dedicated to compassion as well as awareness and wisdom. They took a vow to have compassion and love for all beings. So bodhisattvas lived as part of society, helping others. This opened the door for people with families who worked in the community to become involved in Buddhism.

Another change was in the conception of Buddha. The Theravadins had carried on the tradition of Buddha as a mortal man who created a great system for finding enlightenment. But the Mahayana de-emphasized the person of the Buddha. They saw him as a spiritual presence, an eternal being who appeared as different people at various times throughout history.

The truths that Buddha had taught to his disciples were only a temporary embodiment, not a permanent one. The real truth of enlightenment is wordless, beyond time and space. The Mahayana sutras reflected this change, often presenting enigmatic discourses that led people to a new understanding of reality as illusion produced by the mind and ultimately empty.

Mahayana welcomed many diverse practices for reaching Nirvana. They tried to address the needs of a broad range of people with varying abilities. This open-ended teaching method was called *upaya*, or skillful means. Upaya justified a much broader collection of techniques and methods that could now be used to reach enlightenment. The *Lotus Sutra* depicted upaya with a metaphor of rain that nourishes all varieties of plants and animals:

I preach the Dharma to beings whether their intellect
Be inferior or superior, and their faculties weak or strong.

Setting aside all tiredness,
I rain down the rain of the Dharma
(Conze 1995, 140).

The Madhyamika School (A.D. 200)

Two major schools of Mahayana Buddhism took form, first *Madhyamika* and then *Yogacara*. Nagarjuna's (A.D. 200) thinking and teaching was foundational for Mahayana, and his revolutionary thinking led to the Madhyamika School. Nagarjuna was a philosopher who understood logic and the theory of truth and knowledge. He is claimed as a patriarch of Mahayana and is especially important in Zen Buddhism and Tibetan Buddhism. Nagarjuna's carefully thought-out philosophy became a basis for many later Mahayana schools. His work investigates how we know what we know, a branch of philosophy known today as epistemology. Nagarjuna was clear in his thinking and paradoxical logic, skeptical of any and all theories as valid to guide the mind to enlightenment. His philosophical method was to demonstrate that all claims to or knowledge of logical truth are contradictory, relative, and arguable; therefore all theories of truth are false. Only emptiness remains as the beginning, the zero point in the middle. This nontheory became known as Madhyamika.

As Madhyamika evolved, it divided into two types. One form remained radically skeptical of all theory and encouraged a perspective of deconstruction. In other words, all experience should be viewed without any theoretical constructs, since all constructs are based on false logic and illusion. Candrakirti, a seventh-century Indian Buddhist monk, carried on this branch of Madhyamika. He combined the bodhisattva ideal with

Nagarjuna's skeptical approach, so that a deep source of valid truth could be found in ethics and morality.

The second type of Madhyamika philosophy accepted a theory of the Middle Way with emptiness as its foundation. The Middle Way is the path between all positions, wordless and empty, to be understood only through meditation. The interrelationship between the radical skeptics and the Middle Way theorists led to further developments in later schools of Buddhism.

Yogacara School (A.D. 400–1100)

The next major theoretical school to influence Buddhism's Mahayana evolution was the *Yogacara* philosophy, also known as the Mind-Only, or Consciousness-Only, School. Two brothers, Vasubandu and Asanga (A.D. 400), both Indians, carried forward a movement in Buddhism that was to lead Mahayana in a new direction. Together, these two brothers developed an application of consciousness theory known as Yogacara, also called *Vijnavadu*.

Vasubandu was originally a scholar of the older Hinayana doctrine, but he changed to Mahayana. Vasubandu thought through the logical implications of Buddhism, but, in contrast to Nagarjuna's approach, came to the conclusion that the world of appearances was due to a natural function of consciousness—everything comes from the mind; all is illusion. The Yogacara view is positive about the mind's role in reality: Mind is intimately bound in the world of reality, and so a disciplined application of meditation with logic can bring about a higher consciousness, free from distortion.

The Yogacarins believed there is a mechanism of mind called the storehouse consciousness that accounts for the relative stability of reality. The storehouse consciousness holds our ideas and memories of experiences, which then lead to other ideas and further experiences of the world. And each new experience results in more memories of experiences, ideas, and seeds, continuing the process. So these seeds give us the effect of the permanent world we know, based in their interrelationships and resulting concepts. The storehouse consciousness helped to explain the difficult Mahayana conception of our empty and illusory world. This school developed meditation techniques drawn from yoga to direct and focus the mind toward enlightened perception, to free the practitioner from illusion due to the effects of the seeds.

The Yogacarins conceived of Buddha in the new Mahayana way, as manifesting beyond human form as three bodies. This doctrine is known as the *Trikaya* and refers to three distinct levels of Being in which Buddha's spiritual presence exists: the *Dharmakaya*, the *Sambhogakaya*, and the *Nirmanakaya*. Thus, Buddha has transcended the cult of the person in Hinayana to express himself at every level of existence: real, spiritual, and mythical. The Dharmakaya is the absolute level of doctrine, wisdom, and law itself. The Sambhogakaya means the enjoyment body, in which Buddha is in realms with other spiritual beings. This level shows how Buddha exists in mythical and symbolic realms. In the third level, the Nirmanakaya, the Buddha emanates or expresses himself as an incarnation in this world, working to help others. Thus Buddha has always been with us and will continue to appear in the future. These ideas were adopted and developed further by the Tibetan Buddhists.

Mahayana Buddhism Travels

Mahayana evolved as Buddhism spread to other cultures and was drawn into relationship with foreign religions and philosophies. For example, Greek and Mediterranean culture had an influence on Buddhism, particularly expressed in the many sculptures of Buddha.

As Buddhism traveled, it was reinterpreted and melded with indigenous religions, philosophies, and language use wherever it went. So when Buddhism went to China, it was reinterpreted to be compatible with Taoism. This helped the Chinese people to understand and accept Buddhism more easily.

The Buddhist scriptures were translated so the doctrine could be disseminated to many countries beyond its Indian origin. Translation bureaus were endowed by monarchs, which led to a number of large-scale projects. Kumarajiva (A.D. 344–413) directed one of the most important and largest translation bureaus under the royal patronage of Yao Hsing. He supervised hundreds of monks in the translation of ninety-four works into Chinese. He translated and interpreted Nagarjuna's writings, which developed into a Chinese Madhyamika School called the Three Treatise School.

New Schools of Mahayana Buddhism

Every country that received Mahayana personalized it to fit its culture. New schools were formed, tracing their roots back to Madhyamika and Yogacara. Tibet formed its own type of Buddhism, combining it with yoga and *Tantra*. China, being a vast country, formed many different schools of Buddhism, each with its own emphases. *Chan*, *Tien T'ai*, *Hua-Yen*, and Pure Land are some of the main forms that flourish today. Japan has its own counterparts that include many original innovations: Zen, *Tendai*, *Kegon*, and *Shingon*. Although these schools have differences, they all share in the spirit of Buddhism, the Four Noble Truths, the Eightfold Path, emptiness, meditation, and many of the other themes in this book.

Lesson
One

Open Your Mind
with Buddhist
Literature

Nirvana is the realm of Dharmata-Buddha; it is where the
manifestations of Noble Wisdom that is Buddhahood
expresses itself in Perfect Love for all; it is where the mani-
festation of Perfect Love that is Tathagatahood expresses
itself in Noble Wisdom for the enlightenment of all—there,
indeed, is Nirvana!

—Nirvana Sutra in Yutang 1942, 556

How to Study Sutras and Buddhist Literature

We are accustomed to academic learning—which involves mas-
tering a subject matter by accumulating information and memo-
rizing facts. School encourages us to know the discoveries that
have been made in an area by studying what the experts in the
field have to say. Studying Buddhist literature is a different process.

Buddhist literature is a doorway into Buddhism. As students
study and think about the sutras, they are guided into a new

perspective. Sutras don't just contain information to memorize. Nor are the topics based on collections of data. Instead, these works open the mind to a new way of thinking, a nonrational perspective. You become more comfortable with your unconscious, intuitive nature. Correct study leads naturally to meditation.

Buddhist writings are not to be interpreted literally: the words point to an experience beyond words. Sometimes these writings are paradoxical and somewhat mystifying. Similar to looking at a nonrepresentational abstract painting, the writings give you something to react to. You make discoveries for yourself as you experience the images and ideas.

Some Buddhist writings paint elaborate pictures of grand, transcendent scenes that are not to be taken literally, but to be savored for their symbolic effect. Others tell a metaphorical story, to help evoke your associations and teach a lesson. Often they are in the form of a conversation between Buddha and one of his disciples, to provide a you-are-there learning experience.

Using This Lesson

This lesson includes teachings from some important Buddhist sutras and later Buddhist writings. Included are the *Dhammapada* from the Hinayana tradition, the *Prajnaparamita Sutras* from Mahayana, *The Twelve Gates* by Nagarjuna (a later Mahayana work), and *The Scripture of the Golden Eternity* by Jack Kerouac (as a modern example).

The written word is a springboard to stimulate understanding. As you delve into the ideas, open your mind and explore your own experience. Keep in mind that you have just as much potential as any student of Buddhism, and so your own experience can be a guiding light for you.

Setting Buddhist Literature in Context

Buddhism began as an oral tradition, with Buddha's lessons spoken directly to his students. Following Buddha's death, his disciples kept his ideas alive by reciting the sermons from memory. Eventually these lessons were written down in a large collection of literature called the *Tripitaka, the Triple Baskets*. These baskets included the words of Buddha, the rules of the order, and the general precepts for people to follow. Later, commentaries on these original works were added.

The second large body of sutras came later to express Mahayana Buddhism. These writings were said to have come directly from Buddha but had been held back until people were ready to receive them. Historians believe these sutras were actually written between the second century B.C. and the second century A.D.

The sutras themselves are the literature attributed directly to Buddha himself. But a great body of important literature on Buddhism has been written over many centuries. Some of these writings have had a great influence on the course of Buddhism.

Different sects often had a pivotal sutra or treatise that guided the path of the followers. For example, the *Platform Sutra* by Hui-neng changed the course of Zen's history by introducing the possibility for sudden enlightenment to anyone from any background. Fa-tsang's writings helped to weave together the interrelated fabric of Hua-yen's "One is All and All is One" form of Buddhism. But probably one of the most pivotal influences on the course of Mahayana Buddhism was Nagarjuna's works on Emptiness.

Hinayana Sutra: The Dhammapada,
Words of the Doctrine

The *Dhammapada* is a collection of aphorisms in twenty-three verses, drawn from the earlier Hinayana teachings of Buddhism. A number of different versions were collected, but they tend to convey similar meanings. The words are ascribed to Buddha and speak directly to the common person.

The *Dhammapada* begins with one of the central ideas of Buddhism: "All that we are is the result of what we have thought" (Yutang 1942, 328). Cognition is the domain of Buddhism. Changing how you think and what you think about can bring about deep, satisfying happiness. If you honestly make the effort, you can succeed. But you must put your efforts in the right direction. Your real enemy is not your circumstances or other people—it is only your own resistance to changing your own mind: "It is good to tame the mind, which is difficult to hold in and flighty, rushing wherever it listeth; a tamed mind brings happiness" (Yutang 1942, 329).

The main teachings of Hinayana Buddhism are simple to state: "Not to commit any sin, to do good, and to purify one's mind, that is the teaching of all the awakened" (Yutang 1942, 340). But how can people actually achieve these goals? The sutra tells you how. Overcome anger with love. Free yourself from the pleasure and pain of your passions. Unearth the root of your thirst.

The best way to effect these changes is to follow the Eightfold Path. The Eightfold Path, the topic of Lessons Three, Four, and Five, offers guidelines for practicing Buddhism to bring about inner transformation. The sutra states clearly that when you follow the Eightfold Path wholeheartedly, you can get to the root of the problems that stand in the way of happiness. The Buddhas from the past can be guides, but change comes from within you. As you undergo the process, you will share in the perfect wisdom of all Buddhas, Nirvana's complete peace and happiness.

Dhammapada *Contemplation*
What you do and feel results from what you have thought. Contemplate this. Consider the ways that your thinking can influence what you do and feel. Review specific situations and the thoughts you had about them that may have influenced what you felt or did.

Dhammapdada *Mindfulness*
Sit quietly and relax. Pay attention to your thoughts. Imagine that you can watch your thoughts from afar. What do you observe? What sorts of thoughts are you having? Become aware of what you are thinking about. Notice any emotions you are feeling in conjunction with your train of thought. For example, are you feeling happy about exploring Buddhism? Think about any actions you might be considering. Perhaps you are considering making some changes. Gradually allow your thoughts to settle and sit quietly. Can you notice a calming of your emotions as well?

Extend your awareness to everyday life. Try to notice the link between your thoughts, your feelings, and your actions.

Creative Contemplation
Meditate on the other ideas expressed in this sutra. Think about how they apply to your life, your relationships.

Here are a few possible themes:

Hatred doesn't cease by hatred, but by love.
Only you can make change happen.
Don't think lightly of wrong-doing, because it adds up
little by little.

Mahayana Sutra: Prajnaparamita,
Perfect Wisdom Sutras

The Mahayana perspective is expressed in a large group of writings known as the *Prajnaparamita*, or *Perfect Wisdom*, sutras. These sutras express some of the core ideas of Mahayana regarding the wonderful yet elusive nature of enlightened wisdom. Some of the sections are straightforward, while others are paradoxical.

The Importance of Perfect Wisdom

The sutra begins by praising perfect wisdom as the highest and the best of all understandings: "Homage to Thee, Perfect Wisdom, boundless and transcending thought! All thy limbs are without blemish. Faultless those who thee discern" (Conze 1995, 147).

The name of the sutras, *Perfect Wisdom*, implies the content: "The perfection of wisdom is the accomplishment of the cognition of the all knowing" (Conze 1995, 146). The themes in the earlier *Dhammapada* are continued in the *Perfect Wisdom Sutras*: ultimately perfect wisdom can be found in the realm of the mind— so you will not discover perfect wisdom in the external world.

One important sutra included in the *Prajnaparamita* collection, the *Diamond Sutra*, conveys the elusiveness of perfect wisdom by presenting a paradoxical dialogue between Buddha and his disciple Subhuti. The reader who follows the discussion carefully will undergo a change in perspective, an alteration of consciousness. Central to Zen Buddhism, the *Diamond Sutra* cuts through the many illusions people have about the solid, permanent, and real nature of the world. When illusion is cut away, what remains is perfect wisdom:

> Subhuti asked the Buddha, "World-Honored One, is the highest, most fulfilled, awakened mind that the Buddha attained the unattainable?"
>
> The Buddha said, "That is right Subhuti. Regarding the most fulfilled, awakened mind, I have not attained anything. That is why it is called the highest, most fulfilled, awakened mind" (Hanh 1992, 20).

Though one might expect that something so important could be clearly explained and depicted, perfect wisdom is actually elusive. The *Diamond Sutra*, as in all the other sutras in the *Prajnaparamita* collection, explains that perfect wisdom cannot be stated or distinguished or learned. You can't reflect on it with your usual sensing or thinking.

The *Diamond Sutra* is central in Zen Buddhism. You can find a more in-depth description of this sutra with learning exercises in our book *Zen in Ten*.

Emptiness

Why is perfect wisdom so difficult to characterize? The answer is that the true nature of perfect wisdom is empty:

> The wise discern of an act of consciousness the origin and the stopping, the production and the passing away. The Yogin sees that it has come from nowhere, gone to

nowhere, that it is empty, and like unto a mock show (Conze 1995, 159).

The *Prajnaparamita* also presents some straightforward arguments to explain why perfect wisdom is elusive and empty. When we search for the conditions that bring things about, we can't find them. In one example, sound is explored. When we speak, the conditions of our talking are the throat, the lips, the palate, and the rolling of the tongue. But words don't literally come from the throat, lips, palate, or tongue. Similarly, we might then look within the language, grammar, or syntax for where the meanings of our words come from. But when you try to search for the source of your meanings, you cannot find it there either, only a mechanism through form:

> The wise man discerns the rise and fall of speech, or song, or noise, or any sound. They are but momentary and empty. All speech is similar to an echo (Conze 1995, 160).

Unity and Oneness

All the *Prajnaparamita* sutras express how embracing the perfect wisdom of emptiness can change your life. Emptiness frees you from everyday problems because you are no longer dependent on the everyday ups and downs:

> One who in such a way is not captivated by the worldly dharmas is said to be one who knows emptiness (Conze 1995, 163).

When you truly understand the empty nature of everything, you aren't overly excited when things are good, nor are you terribly depressed when things are bad. Fame can't make you conceited or arrogant, and lack of fame can't deflate your ego.

Praise doesn't necessarily win you over, and rejection doesn't necessarily upset you.

Everything takes on a temporary or relative reality through dependent relationships. The sutra gives an example common to the period when it was written: a bucket in a well. Through human effort, grass is twisted into a rope, tied to a bucket, and dropped into a well. The bucket is raised by several revolutions of a wheel. But each revolution, by itself, can't do anything. It is only in the relationship of each action, working together, that water is retrieved from the well. Similarly, everything that happens throughout your lifespan is due to mutual interactions with the world around you. Although the interactions may not always be as clear to you as the example of the bucket in the well, the interactions are just as real.

Modern Contemplation of Dependent Relationships—
Relative Reality

Pick a modern example that might be more relevant to your personal experience than a bucket in a well. You might think about an automobile, a computer, or an electric light. At what point does the group of parts become a whole object? When it functions? If it doesn't work, is it still what it is? Or does it become an object when you can view it as such, or perhaps when others can see it? But what if the others cannot see it or know it as that object? A blind person may not see the light from a light bulb, but does that mean the electric light is not an object? Where are the true limits of the object? Try to understand how any one part is not the whole. It is only through the interrelationship that the machine works as it does and thereby takes on a seemingly separate existence.

Enlightenment in Everyday Life

The *Heart Sutra* is a brief sutra that succinctly states the fundamental ideas of the Prajnaparamita. This sutra points out that form is emptiness and emptiness is form. Absolute reality is not dependent on anything else. It is calm, undifferentiated, without any form—and yet, as it appears in the moment-to-moment world of our experience, form is differentiated, individual, and existing.

The *Heart Sutra* also helps us to realize the implications that result from understanding form as emptiness and emptiness as form. The sutra includes a list of all the ways that there is nothing at the absolute level—no form, no consciousness, no attainment, no pain, no suffering, no body, no emotions, no birth, no death—nothing: emptiness. This realization of emptiness, on a deep level, is perfect wisdom. But emptiness is only part of the understanding. The sutra points out another side to emptiness— that each thing seems to have some unique form on a relative level. In order to truly understand form is emptiness and emptiness is form, you must make a leap of consciousness. When you can recognize both sides, you will achieve perfect wisdom.

Since form is another side of emptiness, Mahayana Buddhism discourages people from withdrawing from the world into the blankness of emptiness. Instead you can and should live an enlightened life by being engaged and involved. Nirvana is not separate from *Samsara*, everyday life. When you have the right mental approach of perfect wisdom, your everyday life is transformed to become truly enlightening!

Form Is Emptiness and Emptiness Is Form Contemplation

Sit quietly in meditation and allow your thoughts to settle. Think carefully about form and emptiness. The sutra states that they are two sides of the same thing, inseparable and yet distinct. Contemplate this. Your understanding of this core topic will evolve as you continue to move through the book. Keep returning to this topic and notice how your understanding deepens.

Later Buddhist Literature:
The Twelve Gate Treatise

Nagarjuna was one of the most significant contributors to Mahayana Buddhism. His thought became integrated into many later sects in China as well as being pivotal to Tibetan Buddhism. Nagarjuna's *Twelve Gate Treatise* is a concise work that lays out twelve arguments as reasons for why logic is not convincing to use for comprehending the nature of reality, leaving only emptiness. Nagarjuna intended the gates to be an entry into emptiness as a foundation: "To explain emptiness and enter into its meaning one should use the Twelve Gates" (Nagarjuna in Cheng 1982, 29).

Nagarjuna's earlier work, the *Middle Treatise*, was largely an argument with the older Hinayana tradition, trying to set out how Mahayana differed. The *Middle Treatise* laid the groundwork for emptiness with an eightfold negation: no origination, no extinction, no permanence, no impermanence, no identity, no differentiation, no coming, no departure. *The Twelve Gate Treatise* works with the first negation, origination. By showing how nothing exists from the beginning, it follows according to Nagajuna's logic that none of the other seven negations that follow could exist either.

Nagarjuna's skeptical argument is fairly simple to understand. He states that we know things in our world by their nature, characteristics, and function. But the existence of nature, characteristics, and function cannot be established without a doubt. For this reason, we cannot be absolutely sure that things exist.

Nothing Exists Outside Its Circumstances

Nagarjuna believed that there is no nature inherent in things. Rather, a thing's nature is dependent on other circumstances. The following two examples help explain:

> At room temperature, mercury is a liquid that is very sensitive to changes in temperature, and so we use it in thermometers—but only in certain circumstances. When greatly heated, mercury becomes a poisonous gas and is unusable in a thermometer. Its nature is not inherently to be used as a thermometer under all circumstances. It varies relative to the circumstance: it needs certain parameters of temperature range.

> The compound we think of as automobile antifreeze circulates and keeps a car cooled. But if a leak happens in the radiator, the pressure of the antifreeze fluid in circulation suddenly changes. This change in pressure allows the antifreeze to heat up and then the engine suddenly overheats. The antifreeze, which should keep the car's running temperature constant, paradoxically boils and heats the engine up. Antifreeze's stabilizing properties are only true in certain circumstances, at certain pressures.

Upon careful consideration, these two examples are fairly self-evident. In both cases, the surrounding circumstances (temperature and pressure) greatly influence the substance. Nagarjuna argues that the same logic applies to all things, even to ourselves: Nothing exists outside its circumstances. Relationships are part of the essence of the object.

Nothing Has an Inherent Function

Function is another way people try to determine the existence of something. We know things by what they do. But Nagarjuna argues that there is no function that is always inherently true for an object. For example, you wear a rain jacket to stay warm and keep out the water, so you might think that keeping people dry and warm is its function. But if you don't take a rain jacket off right away when you come indoors from a rainstorm, the jacket will make you wet and cold. The rain jacket's function is clearly not fixed under all circumstances.

Logic Leads to Emptiness

Having shown how nothing has any fixed characteristics Nagarjuna believes emptiness logically follows:

> All things are empty. Why? Because things have no nature.
> As it is written,
> By observing that the characteristics [of all things] change
> We know all things are devoid of nature.
> Things which are devoid of nature are also non-existent,
> so all things are empty. (Cheng, 1982, 89).

Nagarjuna also explains that although all things are devoid of nature and nonexistent, this is not the same thing as nonbeing. He is not saying that nonbeing is true and being is false. Emptiness is neither being nor nonbeing: "A right view is not a view in itself but merely an absence of views" (Cheng 1982, 21).

Taking any position as to existence or nonexistence, being or nonbeing is impossible. Nagarjuna encourages us to let go of all points of view about reality and hold no view at all. The middle path is the absence of any position. Emptiness is tranquil and still. It is Nirvana.

Contemporary Buddhist Writing:
The Scripture of the Golden Eternity

Modern students of Buddhism have also expressed their understandings in writings. Jack Kerouac (1922–1969), famous for his book *On the Road* and his central role in the beat generation, became involved in Buddhism and composed a work on the subject in 1960 called *The Scripture of the Golden Eternity*. In it, he expressed the Buddhist ideas of emptiness, no-self, impermanence, and Oneness as he understood them. Kerouac's sutra is a beginning on his path to Buddhist enlightenment. His creative glimpse hints that even non-Buddhists can partake in the Buddhist spirit and find transcendent meaning that will apply to living. From his contemporary context he beautifully captures the essence of Buddhism in a way that speaks to modern culture. From his contemporary context he beautifully captures the essence of Buddhism in a way that speaks to modern culture by comparing the world to one all-encompassing movie. His analogy shows how we are part of the same story, interacting together.

Kerouac saw emptiness as reassuring and comforting. Knowing that we are all part of the same stuff, here and not here, in the same way can relieve us of the suffering we undergo from striving for something different than what is. The recognition that form is emptiness and emptiness is form tells us that we are here forever and also not here at all. Life can be good just the way it is. Kerouac points to a moment when his cat is asleep indicating a moment of calm and you can think of your own moment, and feel reassured.

Kerouac understood the Buddhist idea of selflessness, not as a loss of identity or individuality, but as being a unique individual, as you are. Without self-conscious preoccupation, be fully immersed in life as it is. He used an example of a butterfly. The butterfly doesn't feel proud because it reflects the sunlight as it flies through the trees, it just flies. So you too can enjoy the warmth of the sunlight along with everyone else in the world.

Your everyday world can become a means of finding enlightenment. Your own momentary existence can be a source of wondrous and beautiful experiences. Although the world gives no evidence of its existence, as Nagarjuna pointed out, you can attune to the empty silence that continues through the ages. Silence is at the core of everything, coming from the silence of your calm, clear, meditative mind.

Silence Meditation

Sit quietly and close your eyes. Turn your attention to the sounds around you. Notice the space between sounds, the silence behind and around the sounds. Can you get in tune with the silence that is also present? You will notice that wherever you go, there is always silence somewhere in the background. Now empty your mind and discover the silence that is already there. Do this meditation in various settings at different times and you will begin to notice the common denominator—silence.

Compose a Buddhist Writing

Create your own personal statement about Buddhism. It could be in the form of a poem, a picture, an essay, a song, or any other artistic medium. Try to capture and express your understandings following a meditation session. Think deeply and let your ideas flow. Try not to be intellectual or explanatory. Instead, describe your experience as it relates to Buddhism. After you have finished it, set it aside for a while, perhaps a few days, and then contemplate it, using Buddhist principles of understanding.

Buddhist literature is a rich resource. If you want to do a more extensive study, find one of the many translations that are available and read them for yourself. We are fortunate to live in a time when scholars have translated a great deal of Buddhist literature. You will notice how translations vary, showing that much of the wording is open to interpretation.

Keep in mind that sutras are only part of learning Buddhism. Ultimately, Buddhism is experienced from within. Turn to the next lesson to continue your journey.

The Four
Noble Truths

The Core of Buddhism

We are all on a journey,
The path of life.
But when we get lost,
Where is the light?
　　　—C. Alexander Simpkins

We live in a time filled with possibilities. We know that the promise for happiness is at hand. Yet often we are troubled even in the midst of potential. Buddhism guides us on a journey that teaches how to exercise our human abilities to their fullest. This straightforward path, called the Four Noble Truths, helps us take command of our destiny and find deeply meaningful, satisfying happiness. The Four Noble Truths seem to be fairly simple and straightforward, but their meaning is deep and far reaching.

Here are the Four Noble Truths simply stated:

First Noble Truth: Recognize and face the suffering in life.
Second Noble Truth: Recognize the roots of suffering.
Third Noble Truth: Explore how to put an end to suffering.
Fourth Noble Truth: Define a method that will lead to an enlightened life, happy and free from suffering.

Why Are the Four Noble Truths Important?

The Four Noble Truths are the fundamental teachings of Buddhism. They are the topic of the first lesson Buddha taught following his enlightenment. Most forms of Buddhism include these truths as their foundations of practice, although interpretations vary somewhat.

The Four Noble Truths have relevance to all humanity. They realistically explore the roadblocks of life and then show how to travel well beyond them. These four truths not only give a point of departure for understanding but also offer an efficient vehicle for making the journey.

Learning Firsthand

Buddha discovered his insights from his own first-hand experience, and he encouraged all his followers to do the same. Real and lasting change must come from inner exploration. In this way, each person can become a Buddha, an awakened being. Buddha expressed this clearly:

I tell you that if I have not experienced directly all that I have told you, I would not proclaim that I am an enlightened person, free from suffering (from *Discourse on Turning the Wheel of the Dharma* in Hanh 1998, 239).

We invite you to do your own inner exploration. Think deeply on the ideas presented here and try to understand them for yourself. Relate them to your own life, your own experiences. Be open-minded and you may experience a shift in perspective, a new way of thinking. Ultimately Buddhism is your own experience to be discovered in your own way. Enjoy the process!

The First Noble Truth

The First Noble Truth states that life is suffering, not just in the narrow sense of pain or discomfort, but as a broader, existential condition. Buddha specified six kinds of universal suffering:

1) Suffering begins with the trauma of birth.
2) Throughout life we all must deal with the pain and discomfort of sickness.
3) Old age inevitably comes with its infirmities and limitations.
4) The ever-present fear of death is always there.
5) Throughout life we suffer when we have to be involved with things we dislike.
6) We suffer when we are separated from what we love.

The first step on the Buddhist path is to face our painful existence by accepting and even embracing what is. People typically think it is better to try to avoid suffering by ignoring or denying it. But paradoxically, the more you try to ignore discomfort, the more uncomfortable you become. For example, if you cut your finger and ignore it, the cut often becomes infected and gets worse. But when you clean it, treat it with an antibacterial compound, and cover it, the cut quickly heals.

Facing suffering applies to psychological discomfort as well. Effective psychotherapy helps people to face and accept suffering as part of the change process. When people feel an uncomfortable emotion, their first instinct is often to avoid or ignore the feeling. But this strategy can be ineffective if the feeling needs attending to. Avoiding an uncomfortable feeling may make the discomfort worsen. Psychotherapy guides people to sensitively pay attention to the suffering they feel without judging it as good or bad, but just feeling what is there. Psychotherapy clients pay close attention to their suffering and then are surprised to discover that these feelings transform. Eventually, discomfort eases. Clients usually leave the therapy session with a deeper understanding of themselves and the root of their suffering. As the Dalai Lama said, "If you directly confront your suffering, you will be in a better position to appreciate the depth and nature of the problem" (Cutter and the Dalai Lama 1998, 136).

Complete freedom from suffering is possible. So as you face suffering in the Buddhist way, keep in mind that you are not just indulging in negative thinking. In becoming aware of your suffering, your intent is to transform it for the better.

The Second Noble Truth: The Roots of Suffering

The Second Noble Truth is to recognize that there is a basic cause of suffering: self-centered desires. The problem with selfish craving is that it tends to take over and compel us on a narrow course, limiting our potential. By looking deeply into the nature of selfish craving, how it comes about, and how it affects you, you will begin to understand how suffering takes form.

But what is it that we are really seeking? People are looking for lasting satisfaction for themselves. If you take a step back and reflect on this, you can see that much of what people do is influenced by efforts to find personal pleasure.

Some may argue that seeking lasting personal satisfaction doesn't seem like a bad way to live. People often form a personal goal, something they want to have or achieve, and then they go about trying to get it. There are many meaningful and happy experiences in life, especially in our modern times when we have so many fulfilling ways to spend our time. But somehow, lasting satisfaction evades our grasp. Even people who seem to have everything they want often feel unhappy. This is a paradox. Why wouldn't satisfaction of desires and wishes bring lasting pleasure?

Impermanence

Buddha had an answer for this paradox. He believed that even the happiest times inevitably come to an end. Nothing lasts forever. So we cannot help but be disappointed when we long for what we cannot have. Impermanence is the other side of existence. Change is in the very nature of all things. Our world as we know it is altering continuously. In this way, it is empty of any fixed existence.

This impermanent quality of existence leads to suffering when people expect things to last. We want to keep the good things, so we create the illusion that things will last forever. For a time they do. We use various strategies to hide impermanence, but these methods will not work for long. Trying to avoid impermanence is like the task of Sisyphus, who was doomed to push a heavy boulder up a hill, only to have it roll back down when he nearly reached the top, forcing him to start again.

In order to travel the Buddhist path, you must face the nature of change. When you understand impermanence, you can begin to move toward fuller happiness. The three exercises that follow can help you to experience impermanence. Try them all to discover which one or ones make sense to you. Just as you can't quench your thirst without literally swallowing water, you won't be able to understand Buddhism without personally thinking about the ideas.

Contemplating Impermanence

Begin contemplating impermanence by thinking about the many changes happening around you. Pick an example of change you have noticed in your own life. For example, perhaps you were reunited with a friend you had not seen for many years and were struck by how much that person had changed. Or maybe you have noticed how your neighborhood has altered over the past few years.

Expand your thoughts about change. Consider how the world has changed over the past one hundred years. Think back two hundred years, then a thousand years. Now consider how the earth has transformed over ten thousand years, one hundred thousand years, a million years. Consult an encyclopedia or resource book to help make this more vivid. Now consider how the world will change in a hundred, two hundred, a thousand years. Can you imagine how the world will be different a million years from this very moment?

Experiencing Impermanence with Breathing

Sit down on a small pillow on the floor. Cross your legs and hold your hands comfortably in your lap. If you are not comfortable sitting on the floor, sit in an upright chair and let your feet rest flat on the floor. Turn your attention to your breathing. This means to become aware of your breathing in and out without altering it: Simply notice how you draw air in through your nose, down into your lungs, and then out again. Can you perceive how each breath ends and then a new breath begins? Even though it seems like breathing is one continuous ongoing process, it really is separate and unique breaths, lasting but an instant.

Experiencing Impermanence with Thinking

Turn your attention to your thoughts. Notice what you are thinking right now. Notice how one thought begins and then ends. Then another thought begins and ends, and then another. Your thoughts are probably associated, one to the next, but try to recognize how each thought is unique and separate with but a brief existence. Even if you think about the same idea over and over, each revisiting of the idea is a new thought, somewhat different. Can you experience the impermanence of thoughts as they come and go?

The Third Noble Truth: Putting an End to Suffering

The Third Noble Truth teaches how to stop creating suffering by refraining from doing the things that cause it. Buddha taught the Middle Way between extremes, the way of moderation. The Middle Way means more than just avoiding extremes. On an existential level, the Middle Way also means to not become entangled in the duality of pleasure and pain.

People believe that pleasure is good, something to strive for, and pain is bad, something to avoid. But if all things are ultimately impermanent and illusory, then simply seeking pleasure and avoiding pain is a trap. In pursuing pleasure we are looking for something that we can never have for long. In avoiding pain, we are doubling the discomfort with our own judgments and worries about it. We may become so caught up in our own interpretations that we lose touch with the true nature of the experience itself.

The way to overcome suffering is to let go of craving for pleasure and hating to suffer. This acceptant attitude leads to freedom from the ups and downs of life that are often experienced as so disturbing. Life becomes just what it is, moment to moment.

Appreciate Things as They Are

Think about a simple pleasure you have had in your own life, such as enjoyment of a flower. Can you appreciate the pleasure for what it is and enjoy it fully, without expecting to keep it forever? Expand this attitude to a more involving pleasure, perhaps from a meaningful relationship. Can you appreciate the relationship as it is now, and make every moment count? Realize that even though you both keep changing over time, you don't have to fear change. Each moment is different and can be appreciated and enjoyed for what it is now.

A good example of the importance of living moment-to-moment is the experience of growing up. Each phase of life is different, with its own satisfactions and enjoyments. What pleases a two-year-old would not be pleasurable for a child of ten or fifteen. Teenagers and adults are satisfied by different things—a teen might like loud music, a tired mom might like peace and quiet. If you try to attach yourself to any one phase of your life, you get stuck. Appreciate each part of life for what it can bring, and then move on.

Exercise in Getting the Most out of the Moment
Do a task you usually don't like doing, but approach it differently from usual. This time, do it without any preconceived feeling about it. Choose to do something such as washing the dishes, washing the car, vacuuming the rug, or fixing an appliance. Notice the sensations you have as you work. For example, if you are washing dishes, feel the warm, soft, sudsy water. Enjoy the gleam of each newly cleaned dish. Don't leave your concrete experience of the moment by assessing whether you are working too hard, what kind of job you are doing, or if you like doing it. Just be fully engaged. Stay with each moment. Do the work fully. Upon completion, you may be surprised to discover positive aspects beyond what is usual.

Using Attention to Transform Suffering
Pay attention to a discomfort or pain. Be sure to deal with it medically first. Then, sit quietly. Close your eyes and turn your attention to the discomfort. Notice the sensation without judgment, meaning don't tell yourself that the pain is awful or you can't stand it. Instead, simply notice the sensation. Is it warm, cool, large, small, sharp, dull? Stay with it and accept it as it is. You will begin to notice variations. At some moments you might feel the sensation weaken or alter. Notice how pain is not just one blast of discomfort but a number of subtle sensations. Try to relax for a few minutes and then open your eyes and stretch.

Personal versus Universal Pleasure
Another root of suffering comes when we ignore Oneness. We are all part of a greater whole. The personal self is unified with everyone and everything else. For example, a stone thrown into a pond sends ripples throughout. If something happens in one

country, the whole world is affected. Whenever we try to ignore the greater whole for our own personal satisfaction, we narrow and limit ourselves: "Fools to suppose that imprisonment can bring release!" (Smith 1991, 103). By reaching beyond narrow self-interest, a world of opportunity and wholeness opens up. We need to include others for more complete happiness.

You can observe this principle of Oneness by analogy. If you have ever had your own fish tank, you know that the environment you create with its water temperature, bacteria levels, rocks, and plants are all very important to the life of every fish within it. If any one element is off, the whole environment is affected. Like the Zen Buddhist koan, "If the cows of Eshu are well fed, the horses of Ekishu have full stomachs" (Simpkins 2003, 43–44). Everything and everyone is unified, working together in a coordinated whole. Live with love and compassion for all beings. In this way, deeper, fuller satisfactions are gained and suffering disappears (see lesson ten).

The Fourth Noble Truth: The Eightfold Path

Buddha recognized that understanding is not enough. Truly overcoming suffering requires alterations at every level of thought, action, and lifestyle. Buddha offered a program to follow, called the Eightfold Path. When you enter on this path, you go through a transformational journey. You will know yourself more deeply and get more out of every aspect of your life. As you forge your Oneness with the greater whole, your emotions mature. You can find your way along the Eightfold Path by turning to lesson three.

The Eightfold Path

The Method of Travel

The Eightfold path is that path which opens the eyes, and bestows understanding, which leads to peace of mind, to the higher wisdom, to full enlightenment, to Nirvana.
—Sermon at Benares, in Yutang, 1942, 360

We are accustomed to training in order to gain a specific skill such as a skill needed to perform a job, a sport, or an art, but people do not usually think of training general skills for life itself. Life can be improved by developing certain specific skills and life can also be enhanced by cultivating general skills. Some psychologists believe intelligence is a function of specific abilities, while other psychologists think intelligence is one general ability. Taking these two views into account, an effective method for self improvement should work on the specific and general levels. The Eightfold Path is a training method that does both: It works on many levels including mind, emotions, behavior,

Returning to the Village, artist unknown. Eighteenth century, Ch'ing Dynasty (1644–1911), Chinese. Ink and color on silk. San Diego Museum of Art.

lifestyle, and ethics, targeting specific improvements along with generalized enhancement.

The Eightfold Path is Buddha's method for complete transformation. Following the path lifts the fog that hides your potential. This lesson will guide you on your Eightfold Path. Buddha was careful to clarify that the Eightfold Path is open to all people, even those who have made mistakes or gotten involved in a negative lifestyle. Anyone who makes the effort can change.

Take the Middle Way

The Eightfold Path is the method of moderation, a middle way between extremes. When people live extremely they pay a price: their minds may not function well. For example, most people have experienced how thoughts become sluggish and dull after overindulging in a large meal. Conversely, when people undergo too much self-denial, such as from crash diets, they may become light-headed and confused.

Taking the Middle Way doesn't mean that you have to live a middle-of-the road, dull life. Nor does it mean you can't participate in intense activities requiring concentrated effort. Buddha's path sharpens the intellect and sensitivities as it develops the body to function optimally. You can't light a fire with rotten wood, nor can you light the fire of your potential with a debilitated body or mind. Following the Middle Way helps you to build vitality and optimize functioning. The Eightfold Path is intended to enhance your development at every level.

As you enter the path, experiment with the exercises at various times during your day. Integrate the Eightfold Path into your lifestyle.

Before You Begin

The Eightfold Path leads you on an inner journey. This doesn't mean that you reject the outer world. The outer reflects the inner just as the inner reflects the outer. Each is part of the other, in relationship, and all are One. As you explore yourself and your world, you will begin to sense the connections. Transformation within will lead to positive changes in your outer situation.

You may find it helpful to keep a journal as you travel along the Eightfold Path. Record what you think and feel and the discoveries you make along the way. Writing in a journal or speaking into a voice recorder may help you to sort out your understandings and to become more aware.

The Eightfold Path Simply Stated

The Eightfold Path involves eight distinctive yet interrelated steps. They are:

1) Right Views
2) Right Intent
3) Right Speech
4) Right Action
5) Right Livelihood
6) Right Effort
7) Right Mindfulness
8) Right Meditation

The Eightfold Path begins by making changes to your inner thoughts, feelings, and experiences, but the effects will naturally spread outward into your world of work, relationships, and creative endeavors. As you progress, you will understand how each one enhances the others and helps you to transform yourself from the inside out.

Right Views

Take the first step on your Buddhist path by developing Right Views. Reflect on your current views, beliefs, and opinions—in other words, your attitudes.

Attitudes are based on the views, beliefs, and opinions people hold. We form many different attitudes as we go through life. Some attitudes are learned from parents, education, and culture. Others are developed from personal experience. Many studies have shown that once formed, attitudes tend to remain stable (Frank, 1991). If you want to change an attitude, it is not just a simple matter of changing your mind, like deciding to have apple pie instead of blueberry pie for dessert. Altering attitudes calls for deeper exploration.

To Begin with Awareness, Examine Your Attitudes

Changing of attitudes becomes possible with awareness of them. Look realistically at your current views about the world. People often have implicit opinions and views that they aren't aware of. Think about your views of change. For example, what are your views about personal change: is it possible or impossible? What is your opinion about the source for change? Does change come from the environment and outer circumstances? Are other people or situations responsible for your problems? Or can you do something about your problems by changing your attitudes toward life? Do you believe people have free will, or are people's actions determined? Can you imagine another

way of being in your life, not just like a boat drifting downstream, but instead, as the person rowing the boat?

Evaluating Your Attitudes
Next evaluate your attitudes. Do your views tend to enhance or
limit you? Do they help or interfere with your positive efforts?
Do they encourage or prevent you from making positive
changes?

Consider whether your views are conducive to a compassionate life. Do your views open the door to awareness or close
it? Buddhism distinguishes between wholesome and unwholesome roots. You can water the roots of wholesomeness just as
easily as the roots of unwholesomeness. Some attitudes tend to
foster positive directions working for you, while others work
against you. Clarify for yourself what views may be "unwholesome" in the Buddhist sense of leading you away from your path
to enlightened living.

Developing Right Views

Buddhism is not an "anything goes" philosophy. When you want
to help a plant to grow you must give it correct conditions—the
right amount of light, water, and nourishment. Similarly, Right
Views will foster your endeavor, and wrong ones will hurt it.
Once you have become aware of your views and have evaluated
them, try altering the ones that are not compatible with the
path you are choosing. Embrace new views that are conducive
to an aware, awake life. So a view that it is a waste of time to
develop awareness would be in conflict with the inner transformation the Noble Truths are encouraging. Or an opinion that
people have no free will and that inner change is impossible

would also tend to interfere with your efforts to walk the Eightfold Path. Question and challenge views that create barriers to self-change and personal growth.

The Eightfold Path begins by taking a different view of the world and of yourself. So to step on the path, take an open attitude toward yourself and the Noble Truths. Perhaps you do not completely agree with or understand the Buddhist ideas, but don't simply dismiss them without further thought. One of the goals is to overcome ignorance, and that takes a willingness to think about your views.

Right Intent

The Eightfold Path engages your emotional side as well as your intellectual side. When you care deeply about something, you will find it easier to follow through, even when faced with obstacles. Wholehearted commitment directed by Right Views propels you in the right direction.

Enhancing Your Intent

Motivation to do something is strengthened when you know that it is possible. You may be reluctant to put yourself into impossible endeavors, but when something is possible, even if it is challenging, you will probably be more likely to put in the effort to achieve it. The Third Noble Truth teaches that enlightenment is possible. Anyone can become wise, happy, and free. Right intent points you in that direction.

According to the Third Noble Truth, there is a solution to suffering. There is nothing to stop you from making the changes you need. Motivation builds as you recognize your potential to be free and happy.

Examining Your Motivation

Examining your intent can help you to discover what your real motives are. This will help you to pursue a wholesome path and prevent you from getting bogged down in unwholesome efforts. For example, many people donate to charity to help others, but their real intent may be what Buddhists consider unwholesome. They may hope to receive personal reward for their charity; therefore, they are still trapped by yearning for permanence. D.T. Suzuki recommended doing secret acts of benevolence to keep your motivation pure and wholesome. Imagine doing a kind act not for personal gain or reciprocation but just because it is the kind thing to do.

Summoning Right Intent

Sit quietly and close your eyes. Picture yourself completely free of all your problems. Imagine that you feel capable and motivated. You are feeling peaceful and happy. You have goodwill for others. What is this experience like? You can draw strength from this possibility, since it is your experience, even if only imagined at this point. Trust your inner potentials.

Right Speech

The Eightfold Path is a journey of greater awareness. The next step on the path is to notice your own speech. What we say to people in conversation is a doorway to what we are thinking. We often talk without really listening. But when you do hear what you are saying, you will immediately gain access to your inner experience. Buddha believed that when you start listening to yourself as you talk, you will be able to make changes in what you say and affect your inner development in a positive direction. Right Speech begins with awareness of what you are saying at the very moment you are saying it.

Becoming Aware of Speech

In an everyday, relaxed conversation, pay close attention to your voice and your words as you speak. Hear the tone of your voice. Listen to your own words. Think about the meanings you are trying to communicate. Do your words truly reflect your inner intent? Now observe your listening. Pay attention to voice tones, words, and their intended meaning.

Extend your mindfulness to other conversations in various situations. You may find it more challenging to listen closely when you are in less familiar circumstances. As you listen to yourself and others more mindfully, you may be pleasantly surprised by the many benefits your new awareness brings.

If you have trouble listening to yourself as you talk, try speaking into a tape recorder and then listening to the tape before trying out this skill in actual conversation. You can learn from thinking about what you hear yourself say—and how you say it.

Overcoming Obstacles to Right Speech

Notice anything that might be interfering with your attention to Right Speech. Do your thoughts about other related or unrelated things carry you away? Or do you make judgments and comparisons that interrupt your ability to listen moment to moment? Do you have an emotional reaction that clouds your awareness?

Try to answer these questions without being too hard on yourself. For example, if you find that you have trouble listening to yourself, don't get angry or decide that you are somehow inadequate. The path is one of compassion toward others, and that includes compassion toward yourself. Keep trying with a sincere heart, and you will find that in time, you will succeed in becoming more aware.

Changing to Right Speech

As you pay attention to your speech, you may occasionally hear unnecessary annoyance. Or you may notice times when your words are not completely truthful. Or perhaps you are engaging in gossip. Once you have been able to become aware of your speech, begin trying to alter what you express to others toward greater truth, compassion, and honesty. If you find yourself speaking in anger, stop and ask yourself where the anger comes from. Instead of getting lost in the irritation, stay attuned as you ask yourself if your annoyance might stem from attachment. Think about the Four Noble Truths and try to apply your new understandings of these truths to the situation that is angering you.

Keep in mind that the changes are intended to bring wisdom. So if you lie, for example, you hurt yourself by becoming less in touch with what is really happening. "Each time we give in to this protective tariff, the walls of our egos thicken to further imprison us" (Smith 1991, 107). You should try to do the right thing to avoid ignorance, the real root of suffering. By gently lowering your defenses, you can begin to feel how you are in harmony with the rest of the world. Insecurity, fear, or arrogance tend to dissolve in the process.

Start from where you are. At first you may not be able to completely avoid, for example, gossiping, criticizing, being insincere, or telling unnecessary white lies. But keep making efforts in the right direction. Over time your speech will begin to change. You will notice yourself expressing truth and harmony more often, sure signs that you are on the right path.

Right Action

A right action seems to fill the eye and to be related to all nature. The wise man in doing one thing does all. Or in the one thing he does rightly he sees the likeness of all which is done rightly (Spiller 1965, 200).

Right Action means understanding your behavior and its underlying motivations. Buddha recognized the importance of improving the quality of behavior. Outer actions reflect inner being, and so Right Action is a powerful tool for profound inner change.

You can learn about yourself by observing your own actions and conduct. Psychologists have learned a great deal about human nature by studying all aspects of behavior. In fact, studying mind and behavior is so important that an entire branch of psychology, known as cognitive-behavioral psychology, has made the observation of mind in action central.

The skills you have developed for Right Speech will be useful for noticing your actions too. Just as you can become aware of your speech, you can also become aware of your actions. Change in behavior is begun and sustained with awareness. Begin by paying attention to what you are doing as you do it.

Aid to Awareness: Charting

Psychology has a tried and true technique to help people notice their behavior: charting. Becoming aware of how often and when you do an action can help you to become more aware of it, thereby giving you more control over it.

Get a calendar with space to make notations each day. When you would like to become aware of a particular behavior, mark on the calendar each time that you engage in the behavior. At the end of each day, each week, and each month, add up how many times you engaged in the targeted behavior. Note any accompanying facts, for example, where you were at the time, who you were with, or any other relevant details. You can chart negative behaviors you are trying to decrease or positive ones you are trying to increase.

After a period of time has elapsed, review the data you have gathered. Notice any patterns that may emerge. For example, do you tend to perform the behavior at a particular time of day or day of the week? Are you usually alone or with certain people? Do you have any particular mood at the time?

Studying Your Behavior

Study various types of typical behaviors while you are in the midst of doing them. This may give you additional information for your chart. Also, as you turn your attention to what you are doing while you are in the midst of doing it, you will find that you begin to notice new aspects. Observe your behavior in various circumstances, for example while walking around a store, when getting together with friends, or when you are alone.

Next study the quality of your actions. Do you rush around without thinking about what you are doing? Are your thoughts ahead of your actions? Do you do a sloppy job? Are you overly hesitant? What else do you notice?

Take note of how you behave with others. Are you self-centered in your actions or, do you think of other people too?

Right Action: The Five Precepts

Buddhism has certain fundamentals of behavior called the Five Precepts. These precepts are important guidelines for behavior. Most people will find them a common denominator with other traditions. The precepts are: avoid destroying life, don't steal, never lie, don't engage in sexual misconduct, and don't abuse intoxicants.

Buddha believed that when people engage in wrongdoing, it comes "from motives of partiality, enmity, stupidity, and fear" (Fisher 1994, 117). The source of evildoing is ignorance, not sin. If you are having trouble abiding by any of these precepts, set change in motion by overcoming ignorance. Educate yourself about your problem. For example, if you struggle with an impulse to use intoxicants, learn all about the negative effects on the body and mind. Then try to learn about your own motivations. Apply insights from the Noble Truths. Are you clinging, falsely believing that intoxicants are your source for pleasure? Reconsider your attachment to pleasure and aversion to discomfort. Can you find the Middle Way between? (See lesson 9 for more detail.)

If you have difficulty behaving in accord with these precepts on your own, consider seeking support. A Buddhist temple may offer group meditation and guidance from a monk. You may also decide to consult a psychotherapist. Or sometimes churches will offer pastoral counseling. The precepts are the pathway to a mind free of conflict and disturbance, and seeking assistance may be a positive step.

Making Changes

Right Action is an ongoing process. Begin by trying to avoid the negative behaviors. But this is only one side of Right Action. Try to alter your behavior to become more benevolent. Perform kindnesses whenever you think of it. Begin with random little things, such as giving bread crumbs to a wild bird or helping someone carry a heavy package. Expand your range of kind actions. Try treating acquaintances with courtesy and consideration. Be helpful to friends and family whenever you can. As you become more integrated between thought, feeling, and action, you will find it easier to express your benevolence. (See lesson 10 for more detail.)

Right Livelihood

Buddha believed that people wouldn't become enlightened if they spent most of their day working at a profession that is contrary to enlightenment. Any field that is in direct conflict with the five precepts should not be pursued. Buddha named certain prohibited jobs such as poison peddler and slave trader. Translating his criteria into modern terms is fairly straightforward: any occupation that doesn't harm yourself or other people is compatible with the Eightfold Path. This criterion leaves room for most modern forms of work. Fields that help other people are especially compatible. People who are involved in manufacturing, building trades, and arts are creating something for the use, convenience, or enjoyment of others. Service professions such as medicine, psychology, and public relations are helpful to the world. Business can be positive for the culture as well.

Most occupations have the potential to be helpful when done sincerely and well. But people can turn a potentially positive job in the wrong direction. For example, a merchant who cheats customers always has the choice to stop doing so. Just as much opportunity exists for doing Right Action as for doing wrong action. Some wealthy CEOs help their employees and support numerous charities, while others run their business dishonestly. How you choose to act in your occupation is largely up to you. Of course there are situations where you do not have the free will to do Right Action, and Buddha recommended people should leave such jobs. But usually improvements are possible.

Assessing Your Occupation

Think about your work situation in terms of the Buddhist criteria. Do you have the opportunity to be honest and do your best work? The job may not be perfect, but it should not interfere with your being aware and compassionate.

Making the Most of Your Work Day

Buddhist enlightenment does not just happen on your time off; enlightenment is part of everyday life as you are living it. Enhance your awareness as you go about your day, and you will find that you think more clearly and work more efficiently. Aware in every moment, you can walk the Eightfold Path even at work.

Performing a Work Task with Awareness

Pick a small task you do at work. Before you begin, sit down and close your eyes. Feel your sensations as you sit in the chair. Bring yourself fully into the present moment. Then, when you feel calm and steady, open your eyes and begin to perform the task. Notice everything about what you feel as you do it—how you move, what you think, what you feel. Work efficiently without rushing or lingering. When you are finished, sit down again and again close your eyes. Sit quietly for a moment until you are ready to continue with your day. Try to keep your awareness attuned throughout the day.

Being More Compassionate at Work

You can extend your compassion into the workplace. Try to be considerate and helpful with your fellow workers. Whenever there is a choice between self-centered action and other-centered action, try to plant the seeds of benevolence. You do not act in a vacuum, and your kindness could inspire others. You may be surprised to enjoy the fruits of your actions with a more comfortable and harmonious work environment.

Right Effort

Enlisting the will consists of two features: resolve and attention. Once you have made the decision to do something, attention must be drawn to the thing that you want to do along with a continuing commitment to keep at it. Right Effort means whole-heartedly applying yourself to the Way by optimizing the use of willpower. You can change if you truly want to.

Setting Your Resolve

Right Effort begins with a decision: I want to do this. You have probably noticed that when you really want something, you will usually try to get it. So first, decide that you want to make changes in your life. Choosing to transform your life is a long-range effort with many challenges along the way. Once you have made a decision, set yourself for what you want to do with firm commitment. Right Effort involves setting your whole being for full engagement in the process. The Eightfold Path enlists your thoughts, feelings, words, actions, and livelihood so that you can put forth a unified effort.

Unfortunately, good intentions are not enough. Many people want to accomplish and achieve, but they find themselves stuck in passive patterns. Inertia can be combated by correct use of the will. If you have some negative habits that are preventing you from achieving, you will need to work hard to overcome the force of habit. At first the effort required is intense. Over time, it gets easier.

One of the foremost Japanese Zen monks, Hakuin, devoted himself single-mindedly to his effort to become enlightened. During his first ten years of monastic life, he sustained his meditation practice long into the night, strapping himself upright to keep from falling over in tiredness. Another Japanese Zen master, Dogen, recognized the urgency of making the commitment now:

> Time flies faster than an arrow; life is more transient than the dew. No matter how skillful you may be, it is impossible to bring back even a single day of the past. . . . Each day's life should be esteemed; the body should be respected. It is through our own practice that the practice of the various Buddhas appears and their great Way reaches us (Yokoi 1990, 63).

Making Your Commitment

Think about the ideas you have been reading about and decide to make a commitment to becoming more aware in every aspect of your life. Remember your decision during the day, and act on it. Carry out your commitment whenever possible as you go about your daily routine.

If resistances come up, fight against them. Recognize what the resistance is and try to answer it by doing whatever is needed. Get more information, talk to someone who can be helpful, or think through your difficulty. Get inspiration from true stories of people who have overcome tremendous obstacles. You can accomplish great things if you set yourself fully to do so.

Focusing Attention

Primary in the activation of the will is correct use of the attention. So once you have made your decision, you will need to direct your attention correctly. Actions that have your close attention are more readily carried out. Follow-through becomes easier when you carefully attend to what you wish to do and hold that idea firmly in mind. Training of attention is key. One of the founders of modern psychology, William James, understood this important quality to making successful efforts:

> The essential achievement of the will, in short, when
> it is most voluntary, is to attend to a difficult object
> and hold it fast before the mind. The so-doing is the fiat;
> and it is a mere physiological incident that when the
> object is thus attended to, immediate motor consequences
> should ensue. . . . Effort of attention is thus the essential
> phenomenon of will (James 1896, 561–562).

Attention Warm-up Exercise

Practice deliberately directing and holding your attention. Sit down in your living room and look around. Let your attention move from thing to thing without stopping. Then pick one object and keep your attention focused on it for several minutes. Don't think of anything else; just keep concentrated on this one thing. Keep your mind actively interested and aware of the object you have chosen. At various times during your day, practice deliberately focusing attention. Decide what you will be attentive to, and then do it.

Engaging Full Attention

You can direct your attention to concentrate on your steps on the Eightfold Path. For example, when practicing Right Speech, deliberately direct your attention to your speech. Give your complete attention to an activity you are doing. Don't divide your attention by talking while you are doing something else. Experiment with placing all your attention on the chosen task, whatever that is. You will find being focused in this way adds a new dimension to everything you do.

Unifying Your Efforts

Right Effort unifies all your capacities together. When you can combine actions with thoughts, emotions, speech, and lifestyle, you will begin to change. All of the steps on the Eightfold Path work in conjunction with each other. If you are engaged in Right Action, your mind is directed to what you are doing, your emotions are engaged, and what you say about it is congruent as well. But how can you coordinate everything in this way?

The last two steps on the Eightfold Path, Right Mindfulness and Right Meditation, can help you to integrate mind, body, and spirit together. These skills are so central to the practice of Buddhism that the next two lessons are devoted to them.

Continue on your path with a sincere heart, and you will develop a strong will to bring about the kind of fulfilling life you seek.

Right Mindfulness

The Tool of Awareness

Mindful he breathes in, mindful he breathes out. Whether
he is breathing in a long or a short breath, he compre-
hends that he is breathing in a long or a short breath.
　　—"Mindfulness" in *Majjhima-nikdya I*, in Conze, 1995, 59

A Buddhist master lived in a simple hut far from any village. One
evening the monk was out walking, mindfully aware of his surroundings. Meanwhile, a robber had entered the hut. The robber looked all
around for goods to steal, but could find nothing. Just then the monk
came home and saw the robber. The monk said, "You have traveled
a great distance to visit me. I wouldn't want you to leave with nothing. Please, let me give you the shirt I'm wearing."

　　The robber was puzzled by this strange offer but took the shirt
and left. Then the monk sat down and meditated on the moon,
whose wonderful clear light shone through his open window. "Poor
robber," he thought. "If only I could give him this stunning moon!"

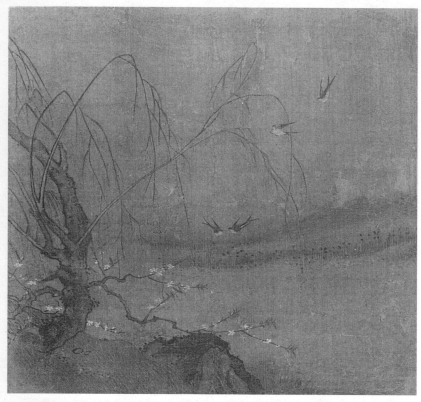

Swallows Flying by a Willow Tree, artist unknown. Fifteenth century, Ming Dynasty (1368–1644), Chinese. Ink and light color on silk. San Diego Museum of Art.

Even though the monk was poor in his material possessions, he had something far more valuable: Mindfulness, which allowed him to be enriched by his everyday experience.

The seventh step on the Eightfold Path, Right Mindfulness is devoted to a classic Buddhist form of meditation known as mindfulness. As you practice mindfulness, you wake up, as if from a dream. Everything becomes more vivid. Daily life takes on deeper meaning. You meet each experience of life wholeheartedly, without hesitation. Like the Buddhist master in the story, you appreciate and enjoy each moment and marvel at the beauty of the world all around you.

The word "mindfulness" implies its meaning: mind-*full*-ness is a method for filling the mind fully and completely with each moment. So mindfulness is not just a matter of what you do, but rather how you apply your mental attention and involvement.

Right Mindfulness is an approach to life, a way of orienting yourself with alert awareness and complete presence. Life without mindfulness is foggy and vague, driven by blind impulse and external pressures. But a mindful life opens a vast vista of potential for wisdom, freedom, and compassion.

Mindfulness begins with you in your own experience, here and now. Work with the exercises to develop your skills. Use your body, feelings, and thoughts. In time, your awareness will spread into every moment, like a light that illuminates the darkness.

Work with the methods presented in this lesson and the next one. Then go back and apply these skills to earlier lessons. You will enjoy how mindfulness and meditation can deepen every experience of life.

Personal Mindfulness:
Taking a Nonjudgmental Attitude

Mindful awareness is nonjudgmental. Like a scientist who is gathering data, you should not jump to conclusions or use the new information you gain from being mindful to form biased opinions. Wait until you have a fuller picture. Trust the process and cultivate an open mind.

Mindfulness gives you the opportunity to get to know about all your life, actions, thoughts, and feelings. But as you learn to observe more deeply, you may not always like what you see at first. As a result, you might be tempted to pass judgment on yourself or others before you fully understand. Moralizing will not help you on your path. In fact, it may interfere.

There is an important difference between observing something that may need changing and moralizing about it. Whenever you can simply observe, you will find that your inner mind opens up to you. So as you begin to experiment with mindfulness exercises, try to observe without making judgmental pronouncements: just become aware of yourself in the situation. If you notice something about yourself that you don't like, take note of it. You may decide that it is a quality you would like to change, but do so without criticizing yourself.

Fostering Mindfulness by Accepting Yourself

You can practice refraining from judgment as you notice details of your experience, your actions, and their effects. Some of the Hinayana sutras encourage people to focus on negative impurities and unattractive physical aspects of themselves in order to train the mind to accept the bad along with the good and cultivate detachment. Try to become aware of what is there, but keep your observations clear and descriptive. Learn to accept your experience of yourself without making comparisons or criticisms. Then you will be able to appreciate your qualities, just as they are.

This might be easy to do if you are handsome or beautiful, with a flawless disposition and no faults, but what if you are not so perfect? Can mindfulness apply to a person who is, for example, confined to a wheelchair, missing legs, or somehow disfigured? Many disabled individuals answer with a resounding, "Yes!"

"Buddhism provides the ideal method for living with a disability: The ultimate triumph of mind over matter" (Bruno, 1999).

Dr. Bruno, confined to a wheelchair himself, encourages people to make positive adjustments to their situation using Buddhism. Many have learned to become fully aware without adding any suffering: to accept and transcend their life situation.

The Zen Buddhist teacher, Lin Chi, often told his disciples that nothing is missing. Our problems occur because we doubt ourselves. Everyone is fully equipped to be enlightened.

Nonjudgmental Self-Observation
Survey yourself from head to toe and recognize all your different parts. Traditionally, Buddhism counted thirty-two body parts, but just observe your own body as makes sense to you. Describe each part to yourself. For example, observe that your hair is long, dark brown, and curly or that your face is round, neck slender, shoulders wide, and so on. But don't add an evaluation, such as unattractive, too fat or too thin.

Next describe your personality. Be factual without passing judgment. For example, I am outgoing, or I am withdrawn. I like people, or I prefer solitude. I like to be active, or I prefer to be quiet. Stick to the facts as you perceive them without making judgments.

Attuning to Body Positioning

Now that you have practiced taking the correct attitude for mindfulness, turn your attention to your body. Start by noticing your body positioning and movement at times while sitting, standing, lying down, and walking. When you are going about your day, take a moment to notice your body sensations. We often pay very little attention to such fundamentals. But our body sensations are part of everything we do, an important and valuable experience to tune in with. So, when you first wake up in the morning, begin by taking a moment to notice yourself lying in bed. Then as you get up, pay attention to how you sit up, step onto the floor, and slowly stand up. Take note of your body positions whenever you have a chance throughout your day.

Mindfulness of Position

Delve a little deeper and pay attention to a certain position. For example, when sitting on a chair somewhere in your house, notice your posture. Are you sitting straight, leaning, or slumping into the chair? Do you take support from the chair or push down on the seat? Where are your feet? Pay close attention to all the details.

The Important Practice of Mindful Breathing

Once you have been able to notice your physical being, you have taken the first steps toward mindfulness. Next, delve into one of the most widely practiced Buddhist traditions: mindful breathing. Yoga also uses breathing as a focus for meditation.

We must breathe to live, but we often do so without paying much attention to the process. By consistently turning your attention to breathing, you have an accessible inroad into your deeper being. Many people find that paying attention to breathing is one of the easiest ways to begin the process of becoming aware.

Mindful Breathing Exercise

Sit on a small pillow on the floor and cross your legs. If you have difficulty sitting on the floor, please feel free to sit in a chair. Let your hands rest comfortably on your legs. Keep your back relatively straight so that your breathing passages are free and unrestricted. Close your eyes and breathe normally.

Notice as you bring the air in through your nose. Feel the air in your nasal passages and then follow the sensation as the air travels down into your lungs. Notice the movement in your chest and diaphragm as the air enters. Next follow the air as it moves out. Note how your diaphragm pushes down as the air travels up and out through your nasal passages. Feel the sensation of air pushing out as it leaves your nose.

Try not to alter your normal breathing. At first you might feel tempted to take in deep breaths, but don't. Continue breathing attentively for several minutes. If you catch your mind drifting away from your breathing, gently bring it back.

You may find yourself naturally relaxing. Your breathing may want to be a little deeper and slower. Allow this process to take place only as it feels natural.

Over time you will be able to develop a feeling of calm and ease from mindful breathing. Your sense of inner peace becomes a resource.

Getting to Know Yourself through Mindful Breathing
Attention to breathing can aid in getting to know yourself on an intuitive level. As you turn your attention to breathing at various times during the day, you may become aware of different qualities to your breathing. For example, when you are hurrying around doing errands, your breathing rate may be quick with short breaths. If you feel tense or anxious, you might feel tightness in your chest or breathing passages. When feeling a strong emotion, your breaths might be deep or shallow. Breathing is probably different late at night from early in the morning. Try to notice the differences and accept them as expressions of your inner being.

Always start from where you are, without trying to change anything. As you sit patiently breathing, changes will happen. Remember that each moment is new, so even an uncomfortable breathing pattern will tend to alter. Turn your attention to breathing for a few minutes here and there throughout the day, and you will gain new intuitive understandings.

Mindfulness of Feelings

Emotions are an important component of living, and so mindfulness must include attention to feelings. Buddhism has a strategy for dealing with emotions in a way that will overcome suffering from uncomfortable feelings and maximize fulfillment from positive ones. Mindfulness is key, with a clear method for applying it.

Feelings can be categorized as pleasant, unpleasant, or neutral. People tend to cling to pleasant feelings and reject unpleasant ones. But this clinging and rejecting sets in motion a secondary set of reactions that interferes with awareness and causes suffering. You will be able to drop the secondary reaction as you become more aware of the feelings themselves, without interpreting them further, leading to more comfortable reactions.

The Impermanence of Feelings

All things are impermanent, including feelings. Buddhism encourages us to think about how feelings are impermanent. From the perspective of impermanence, we realize that feelings, like every other aspect of human experience, are actually a series of fleeting moments. Clinging to a pleasant feeling will inevitably lead to frustration because the feeling always ends. Conversely, trying to avoid an unpleasant feeling will also bring suffering, since you cannot escape from your moment-to-moment experience.

Identify Feelings Exercise

Mindfulness of feelings begins when you can identify the emotion you are having. To start the process, sit down for a moment and close your eyes. Turn your attention inward. Try to put a name to your emotion or mood. Then match the description with what you feel. If it is not quite right, modify your label until you feel satisfied.

Next identify whether the feeling is pleasant, unpleasant, or neutral. As you identify it, try to remain calm. Be like a benevolent kindergarten teacher who watches over her students as they play on the playground. When two children begin fighting, she does not become angry with them. Instead she tries to calmly attend to their needs. Benevolently observe all your different feelings, even the ones you have labeled as unpleasant. By eliminating the secondary aversion reaction to a negative feeling, you will significantly lessen your suffering.

Mindful Attention to Feelings

When you are out of touch, emotions seem to take on a power of their own, pushing and pulling in many directions. Mindfulness puts you in the center of your experience, giving you greater ability to understand and manage your feelings maturely.

Begin by noticing pleasant feelings. Next time you are in the midst of a pleasant experience, take a moment to observe. Feel the accompanying sensations. You may want to sit down and close your eyes. With practice, you will be able to sense what you are feeling without needing to stop.

Next try noticing neutral feelings. Work gradually toward becoming aware of the unpleasant ones. For example, practice being aware of mild annoyance before you attempt to tolerate strong anger.

Feeling is not just one quality, but rather is a collection of different sensations. For example, when you are annoyed you may have accompanying sensations such as butterflies in your stomach or quick breathing. Get to know your feeling and all its accompanying aspects. In time you will be able to notice that even the strongest feeling is a combination of sensations. Notice as many aspects as you can, without judgment. With careful attention, the strength of the emotion tends to ease.

Stay with the feeling, moment by moment. You may notice that it begins to change as you observe closely. Can you experience how each moment is different? The intensity of annoyance you felt earlier may have altered now. Let go if there is a difference. Embrace your feelings now and accept yourself, and you can undergo a transformation. Build your awareness skills first, and they will be ready when you really need them. Mindfulness responds to practice.

Mindfulness of Thinking

Mindfulness of thinking involves observing your own mental processes. Mental processes take on many different forms, filling our minds with one thought after another. At times we think with clarity, while other times our thoughts are confused. Sometimes the mind is filled with emotion, and other times it is completely unemotional. But if you step back and look at the broader picture, you notice that all of these different states of mind are really mental processes. For example, if you look at a flower, the flower you see is really a product of your thinking processes, constructed by your mind. In fact, everything you perceive is partly mentally constructed. Through mindful awareness you can step outside the usual mental constructs that seem to fill each moment.

Mindful Thinking

Mindfulness of thinking begins by first recognizing what you are thinking as you think it. Sit quietly and close your eyes. Notice what you are thinking as you think it. Follow the flow of your thoughts. Be like someone sitting on the bank of a river who watches leaves and twigs flow down the river. Don't jump into the river but stay back on shore observing. Keep observing and letting each thought drift past. If you find yourself drifting downstream with a thought, climb back on shore and resume your observing as soon as you notice.

Impermanence of Thinking

As you become mindful of thinking you might begin to notice how your thoughts come and go. Use this meditation to become aware of the transitory nature of thinking.

Observe your thoughts for a few minutes. Then think about this statement from a Buddhist sutra, "A thought is like lightning, it breaks up in a moment and does not stay on" ("Contemplation of Thought" in Conze 1995, 163).

Thoughts are fleeting as they come and go. Stay with each moment of experiencing, and you will notice how difficult it is to stay with a thought. Thought lacks staying power. Even though your present thought may resemble earlier thoughts, each actual thought is only briefly there, then it is gone. Try to focus on the process of thinking, rather than the content, the thought.

Recognize Mental Construction

We do not usually experience the world directly. Rather we experience everything through our consciousness of it. Neuropsychology has shown that we don't perceive with our senses alone; we also perceive with our brains. Certain kinds of brain damage cause blindness, even when there is no injury to the eyes, which demonstrates that the brain plays a vital role in seeing. Other parts of the brain interact with the sense of hearing, smelling, and tasting.

Thus, when you see a flower, you actually see through your brain's interpretation of the information received from your senses. Your perception involves the meanings you have about flowers, both personal and shared with the culture, as well as your sensory experience of the flower. All the collected meanings, both cultural and personal, are stored in the store-consciousness. New experiences are compounded with the storehouse meanings, resulting in a stable experience. The sense of permanence comes from these mental formations—the concepts, the meanings, the abstractions that endure in your mind (see lesson seven). These formations can work for you or against you, depending on many factors.

Through mindful awareness of your perceptual processing, you can begin to gain insight into how your experience gets constructed.

Contemplating How Experience Gets Constructed

You may be able to clarify the Buddhist principle of mental construction by comparison. Think about a television. You understand what a television is and how to use it. But the layman's understanding doesn't go too far beyond a rudimentary sense of how it works. Broadcast engineers would have a much fuller understanding of the television because they know the engineering principles that make the broadcast possible. What if Rip Van Winkle woke up today and saw a television? His understanding would be very different from yours and even further removed from the engineers. Rip might think the television is a strange box with moving pictures inside, or may be something magical. The object stays the same in all three cases, but the human experience of it is constructed from what is already known. Consider how each perspective is constructed. Think of other examples if this is helpful.

Wholesome and Unwholesome Constructions

Some mental constructions are wholesome, tending to uplift you and bring happiness. Others are unwholesome, leading to suffering and unhappiness. Buddhism categorizes some mental processes as wholesome, such as faith, humility, self-respect, and diligence. Other mental processes are unwholesome, for example greed, hatred, ignorance, pride, and doubt. You can probably think of many others.

Some processes can go either way. For example, diligence is wholesome when it helps you stay with your work, but it can be unwholesome if it makes you endanger your health because you refuse to stop working when the need has passed.

With Right Mindfulness, you first become aware of your thoughts and then consider whether they are wholesome or unwholesome. Look more deeply into each thought and trace it back to its roots. If you have an unwholesome thought, where does it come from? Perhaps it is a learned idea, or maybe a culturally shared one. Or perhaps it comes from your own insecurities. Trace back to the origins for a more complete understanding.

Cultivate the wholesome thoughts and encourage them, but discourage the unwholesome ones. Just as a farmer nourishes his plants with the proper plant food, so you should try to nourish your wholesome thoughts whenever possible.

Mindful in the Moment

Gestalt therapy founder Fritz Perls said that awareness is curative (Perls, 1969). You may be pleasantly surprised to discover how these wise words can be true when you practice mindfulness throughout your day.

Now that you have experimented with various ways of being mindful, bring yourself to the present moment. Scan your body to raise your body awareness. To become mindful of your emotions, observe what you are feeling. Notice your mental activity. What are you thinking or perceiving? These qualities of mindfulness can be done quickly, centering you in the present. Once you are in touch with the moment's experiencing, can you let all this go and just be present without any thought?

Notice how your experience transforms moment by moment. Stay with each moment anew. Whenever you can, at various times during the day, turn your attention to your experience. Get in touch as often as you can. In time, mindfulness will be more habitual. Accepting the flow of life as it comes, you can act in harmony with what is needed.

Right Meditation for a Clear Mind

In touch we become
Through meditation
The true person
From contemplation
The same wisdom
Found long ago
Timeless, beyond space
Within, we go.
        —C. Alexander Simpkins

The eighth step on the Eightfold Path is Right Meditation. It is the culmination of all the earlier steps that have been taken. Buddha believed that the mind is our greatest resource. Through correct use of the mind, we have everything we need to be happy and fulfilled. Meditation is the method that develops the

Two Men Meditating

mind correctly to bring about clarity of understanding. Right Meditation awakens the mind to the potentials that are present in each and every person. When you open your mind to meditation, change becomes possible. Problems dissolve and deeper wisdom emerges.

In the midst of everyday activities, the mind is kept continually distracted with details. People move from one thing to the next without a pause. Even at the end of the day when the mind could take some time to reflect, most people fill their leisure hours with structured activity.

Meditation carries you directly to the depths, steering through the continuous flow of conscious thought, navigating into calm seas, and revealing reality in its crystal-clear reflection. Meditation helps you to experience emptiness and undergo a profound transformation of your experience of the world, to lead to enlightenment.

Meditation is a firsthand method; nothing can substitute for your personal exploration of your own mind. Begin meditating regularly, and you will come to your own profound and meaningful understandings. Delve into your own consciousness with meditative exploration.

People have a stereotype of meditation as sitting motionless on the floor. This is one valid way to meditate, but certainly not the only way. Because your awareness is here and now, always available to you, meditation can be done anywhere, any time. As later lessons will reveal, there are many ways to meditate and many settings for doing so. But people who are new to meditation might find it easier to begin meditating in a place that minimizes distractions. The following exercise guides you through the traditional positions for meditation.

Position Yourself for Meditation

For your first experience with meditation, pick a quiet room, or even a corner of a room, with subdued lighting and a comfortable temperature. You may prefer a shady place outdoors in nature, seated on the grass. Find a time of day when you don't have any demands on you. Wear comfortable clothes that don't bind or constrict. As you get better at meditation, you will be able to sustain awareness in more varied situations.

Some people find it helpful to set the stage for meditation. Mild incense can put you in the mood. A picture or a statue of Buddha might inspire you. Meditation music may also help to gently lead you into greater calm.

If you are comfortable on the floor, use a small pillow to sit on. You probably won't need a pillow if you are sitting on soft grass outdoors. There are meditation pillows for sale, or you can use any small pillow. The pillow not only cushions you, but also takes the strain off your legs.

Sit down on the pillow. The traditional posture is the lotus position, where each foot rests up on the thigh of the other leg. But many people will find this uncomfortable, and so a half-lotus (with one foot resting up on the opposite thigh and the other tucked under) or a simple cross-legged position works just as well.

Let your back be relatively straight, with head facing forward. Muscles should remain relaxed but not slack. Sometimes people will slump forward without realizing. Slouching strains your back and restricts your breathing passages, so keep yourself upright.

Hand placement gestures, known as *mudras*, can have significance. Mudras are traditional ways of holding the hands with symbolic meaning. Although Tibetan Buddhism has developed an extensive vocabulary for the use of mudras, all forms of Buddhism use mudras to some extent. One well-known meditation mudra is to place one hand on your lap, palm facing up and open. The second hand rests on top of the first so that the thumbs just barely touch. This position symbolizes unity, and with the legs crossed, allows for the body to form a continuous circle.

Another mudra commonly used in meditation is to extend the arms outward so that the back of each wrist rests on each knee. The index finger and thumb of each hand touch, forming a circle, and the other fingers are open.

Meditation can be done with eyes open, eyes half closed, or eyes closed. Beginners will find it easiest to close their eyes, since this tends to remove visual distractions. Many Zen practitioners meditate with eyes half open and half closed. But when you are meditating in the midst of everyday life, you will often keep your eyes open.

Concentration

Right Meditation is sometimes translated as Right Concentration. Right Concentration focuses attention, narrowing it down to a single point. By focusing attention, the constant flow of thoughts slows. Concentration is a step on the path to emptying the mind.

Many people have trouble concentrating, but concentration meditations can train you to focus. With practice you will develop the ability to direct your attention when and where you need.

Concentration meditations may focus on breathing, on an outer object, or on an inner image. People vary as to which focal point is most effective. Some people find that attention to breathing is natural and easy for them. People with a vivid imagination often like focusing on an inner image, while other people prefer to look at something real. Experiment with all the different types of concentration meditations. You may find that all the different types can be helpful.

Meditation on Breathing

One of the classic meditations in concentration involves counting your breaths as you breathe. You may feel similarities between this exercise and mindful breathing in lesson 3, since mindfulness does involve a certain amount of concentration and both exercises involve breathing. There are no real boundaries between forms of meditation, since ultimately your mind is always involved. Don't try to categorize. Sometimes people find one form of meditation is easier, at first, than another, so it is helpful to try different variations and feel your own reaction. All forms of meditation can be pathways to more enlightened consciousness.

Counting Breaths

Sit down on your meditation pillow (or chair or grass). Close your eyes. Silently count each breath. A full breath in and out is one count. Count up to ten, and then start again. Counting will help to keep your attention directed to your breathing. If you notice that you have lost count, gently bring your attention back to counting. Sustain your counting for a few minutes. Try to extend the amount of time you can stay focused on counting.

Focusing on an Outer Object

Pick a simple shape, such as a box, ball, simple painting, or sculpture. Place it somewhere you can easily see from your meditation seat. Then sit down and focus all your attention on this object. Think of nothing else. If your attention wanders, bring it back to the object. Remember not to criticize yourself—just gently look again at the object. Notice everything about the object: its texture, color, size, and shape.

Focusing on an Inner Image
After observing closely for several minutes, close your eyes and picture the object in your mind. Keep your attention focused on this image. If you find that you have forgotten some detail, open your eyes briefly to look and then close your eyes again. Keep trying to visualize the image. People vary on how crisp and clear the image will be. Don't worry if you can only imagine a vague representation. Most important is to keep your concentration on your image of the object.

Clearing the Mind
One of the great traditions of meditation is clearing the mind. We fill our lives with activities and our minds with thoughts in the hopes that we will find true happiness. But in the quiet moments, the spaces between, our deeper, true nature can be found. Clarity and understanding emerge. You can discover the calm within through clearing the mind with meditation.

Loosening the Grip of Activity
Clearing the mind begins by stopping your activity—by not doing. This requires a shift in your usual intent. Most waking time is spent doing something. Even when relaxing, you are probably engaged in some kind of activity such as reading a book, watching a movie, getting together with people, or playing a game. But not doing is a step on the path leading to

emptiness. In filling yourself with activities, you may miss what lies deeper.

Not Doing

Sit down in your meditation area. Let your body relax. Breathe comfortably. Don't do anything in particular; just sit. At first you may feel uncomfortable deliberately doing nothing, but not doing is an important inroad into meditation. You might begin with a short amount of time, such as a few minutes. As you become more at ease with sitting quietly, increase the time. You will feel more at ease, relaxed, and calm. Let it happen.

Slowing Thoughts

This exercise is a classic Buddhist meditation. Zen Buddhism uses it as a way to come to a clear, quiet mind. Notice that a clear mind does not come about by trying to suppress your thinking. Rather it happens by naturally and sensitively staying attuned to your thoughts as they go along, beginning right where you are.

Sit quietly for a moment or two as you did in the previous exercise. Then turn your attention to your thinking. Notice the first thought that comes to your mind, think about it for a moment, and then let it go and try to just sit calmly with no thought in mind. When the next thought comes along, do what you did before: notice it briefly, but disengage from it and return to calmly not thinking about anything as soon as you can. Keep noticing each thought that arises, think about it briefly, and then return to no thought. As you stay with this, your thoughts will eventually begin to slow down. The spaces between thoughts will lengthen until eventually you will have periods of clarity.

Using an Inner Image

Some people may find that imagery helps them to clear their mind. A clear mind is like a calm lake, so smooth that it reflects the world all around. When a cloud moves across the sky, the lake reflects it. When the cloud is gone, the lake does not try to hold on to the cloud but lets it go past, reflecting whatever comes next.

A Calm, Clear Lake

Imagine that your mind is like the calm, clear lake. As a cloud drifts past, your mind reflects it and then returns to calm clarity. Keep reflecting the clouds that pass, but always return to the clear lake. After some time, all clouds clear and the lake reflects the vast, blue sky. Stay with the clear lake.

Meditation is a skill that responds well to practice. Perform one or several of these meditations each day. Be patient with yourself. Gradually you will begin to feel changes. Deeper calm, heightened awareness, and greater vitality are a few of the common experiences people have. Be open to your own personal transformation and enjoy the process as it unfolds!

Emptiness Is Marvelous

One who is in harmony with emptiness is in harmony with all things.

—Nagarjuna

One day Subhuti, one of Buddha's disciples, was meditating under a flowering tree, experiencing emptiness. A gentle breeze shook the tree, and its flowers began to fall down all around him.

The breeze seemed to be saying, "We are praising you for your clear statement about emptiness."

"But I haven't said a word," answered Subhuti.

"You have not said anything about emptiness, and we have not heard anything about emptiness. This is true emptiness."

The blossoms showered down on Subhuti as he smiled.

The Empty Frame, C. Alexander Simpkins & Annellen Simpkins. 1999, United States. Mahogony on wenge. Private Collection.

Buddhist Logic

Buddhism is a paradox of logic. Everything is possible and nothing is possible. Emptiness is the basis of Buddhism's different form of logic. When we use Western logic, we know what is taking place when we distinguish between what things are and what they are not. For example, here is a table that I am writing on. If the table weren't here, my computer would fall on the floor! According to logic, this table exists, and it would be wrong to say it doesn't exist. We are using the logic of difference, comparison, and contrast to help determine reality.

But in Buddhist logic, the point of no-point, the center, reveals reality. The center is in perfect balance. Comparison is not useful for determining the being or nonbeing of the object. Instead, from this center, being and nonbeing of an object, a person, or a circumstance appear. Returning to our example of the table, this table that I am sitting at typing is really a combination of many factors interacting simultaneously. The table doesn't exist separately. In this moment, certain forces balance, molecules cohere, such that in this flash of the moment, this table appears. The table doesn't necessarily exist outside of this interconnected moment. Nothing does with certainty. That is an example of emptiness.

Buddhist philosophy includes a theory of knowledge with emptiness as the ultimate reference point. Many Westerners struggle with the Buddhist philosophy of emptiness, which seems counterintuitive and hard to understand. But if you open your mind, you will begin to comprehend this important idea.

What Emptiness Is Not

Emptiness may be easier to understand if you think about what it is not. Emptiness is not like a void or vacuum in the material world. Nor is emptiness a thing. It is the absence of individual things as independent of everything else.

Longing for a state of being is not emptiness. It is not a negative quality, like something that is missing and should be there. Emptiness is not some*thing*. To not be is just as mistaken as to be, in this way of thinking. Don't think of emptiness as a view of reality. If you try to look for an ultimate reality, you will only find emptiness.

Emptiness is not to be feared. It is neither good nor bad. Emptiness is not irrationality and chaos any more than it is reality and order.

What We Can Say about Emptiness

Emptiness manifests in many ways. Buddhist doctrine is skeptical of a real, objective world, and it doubts all theories of reality. No theory is irrefutable. Since no inner nature, characteristic, or function can be established, objects as tangible substance in the world cannot be said to exist.

Therefore, everything is empty. Emptiness is the fertile ground for all that is. It is the shared essence that puts everything and everyone on equal footing. Because of emptiness, everything is possible. Emptiness is the essential core, the precondition for the world we know.

If we examine how a thing works as a criterion for the inner nature of something, nothing enduring is found either. For example, when a car develops problems, at what point does the car stop being a car? If it stops running and doesn't work at all, is it no longer a car? Or does a nonworking car remain a car, just one that doesn't work? At a certain point, we may begin to call it by another name, such as "a piece of junk." But to a skilled mechanic, the non-working vehicle is still a car, just a car with a problem to understand and solve. So what is a piece of junk to one person is still a car to another.

Objects have a dependent existence, moment to moment, a temporary existence. But no timeless essence in a material world of reality actually exists. Things don't just stop existing when they don't function or are outdated. Instead, objects change, moment to moment. The relationship between an object's elements and its use is all that is really there, with no timeless essence apart from the interdependency.

Empty Ego

The self, also called an ego in Buddhism, is impermanent, ever changing, and without substance. This understanding has great potential to free us from the fetters of a limited self-concept and narrow self-concern:

> Realization of egolessness is not something negative
> like losing one's self-identity, but rather is positive in that
> through this realization one overcomes one's ego-
> centeredness and awakens to Reality (Abe 1995, 213).

Buddhism's specific concept of an empty self-nature is an extension of emptiness in general. We all share in the same inner empty nature. So the loss of belief in our ego-centered existence lets us discover our deeper true nature, at One with the greater universe, our Buddha Mind.

Empty nature does not mean a loss of individuality. Everything exists at each moment, uniquely as it is. Although we inevitably change and evolve along with the world of which we are an intimate part, we are unique individuals in every moment.

Contemplation of Empty Self

Think about the person you are right now, wherever you are. Then think back to how you were yesterday at work or school or at the store. You will probably notice some differences. Of course you will also note a sense of continuity from day to day. But if you jump back in time several years to different con-texts—perhaps before you started a job, a marriage, or a new school—you will begin to see larger differences. Even though you are always you, you will not find an enduring fixed self-concept. You will find many. Can you open yourself to the possibility that you may be more than your concepts about yourself? Concepts are limiting, but emptiness is infinite.

Emptiness as the Middle Way

The multitude of things that seem to exist are actually impermanent experiences, empty of any true existence. But even though things don't really exist in a lasting, absolute sense, they do have a temporary existence. The world of reality is more than mere appearance. It is there momentarily, in the present moment, just not for all time. Since everything is ultimately nonexistent, but also temporarily existing, a Middle Way, or mean, comes into being.

The Middle Way is a shift in perspective to the center. Seek the balance point. When you return to the center and work out a solution from there, you are not trapped by narrow biases, and you do not need to avoid potential problems. For a moment, stay in the center and let go of commitment to any particular perspective. From the foundation of the neutral center, you can build a new adjustment. Then change is possible.

Empty Standing

Stand with your feet shoulder's-width apart and arms hanging comfortably at your sides. Close your eyes and rock gently forward and back, carefully sensing your balance. You will notice that exactly at the center point, when you are perfectly aligned with gravity, your muscles are most at ease and comfortable. When you go past the center, your body tightens slightly. Shift back and forth slowly until you find that exact center point where you are most relaxed. Then shift side to side, first over the left foot and then over the right. You will notice again that when you pass the center, your body tightens up. Shift side to side until you find the effortless center point. Stand quietly, allowing your relaxation, empty of effort. The empty center is always there to be experienced from within.

Empty Yourself in Action

Have you ever been so engrossed in doing something that you forgot yourself for a time? Most people have had such experiences when playing a game, doing a sport, reading a great book, or working hard on a project. These are moments of emptiness, when you just do what you do without obstruction from self-conscious concerns.

Empty Action

Meditate before you begin an activity that you like to do. Then involve yourself deeply in that activity, without self-concerns. Be fully focused on what you are doing, with nothing else in mind. Keep your mindful meditative attention on what you are doing until you are finished. Then sit again and meditate until you feel your readiness to stop.

Dependent Co-origination

Buddhism has an answer to the age-old question: Which came first, the chicken or the egg? The Buddhist answer would be that both did! This answer is possible because of dependent co-origination. The world of appearances results from the relationships between its elements. Everything exists together in a single moment, in an interrelated web. Objects, people, and events have no independent existence, outside of their relationship with each other.

Dependent Co-origination Contemplation

Sit down in the center of a room. Pick one upper corner of the room at the ceiling and look at it. Consider how this corner is the result of all the other parts of the room: the walls, the ceiling, and the floor. Think about the parallels with the idea of dependent co-origination.

Next, imagine that the room is destroyed and only the corner is left standing. You would still know that the corner comes from its relationship to the original whole.

Although the entire web of momentary existence is ultimately empty, it does exist for a flash, a moment of time. Then everything is gone, changed into another web. That moment of time is significant and real, but not lasting. Like a cloud of particles in a wave, our world of relationships comes into being and then goes out of being. We cannot stop time, and we don't need to.

In that moment everything exists dependent on everything else. Thus everything we do has an effect far beyond what we might imagine. Our world of meanings is always related to the objects, events, and people we interact with, and beyond.

Grasping the Moment

You can experience the moment-to-moment change in events by attuning to your breathing. Even though breathing seems like one continuous blur, it really consists of separate moments, one following the next, with a fresh breath taken in and pushed out. Each moment is new, slightly different from the last, yet in that one moment, all exists together just as it is.

Grasping the Moment Just as It Is

Sit comfortably in an upright meditation position. Close your eyes and focus on your breathing. Notice how each breath is a new breath, completely separate from the one before. Notice how there are a number of interrelated events involved: your own respiration system that moves the air in and then out, the outer environment of air that you breathe, the floor or chair you are sitting on, the walls of the room surrounding you, the street you are on. Pay close attention.

All of this exists in this moment in just this way. Perhaps in the next moment someone will walk into the room, the telephone will ring, or a car will drive by outside—then this is a new room, a new street, a new breath for you to experience fully.

One Man's Nausea Is Another Man's Nirvana

When we recognize that our world of objects is ultimately empty, devoid of substance and permanence, we may feel uncomfortable and suffer. We may suffer as we see, hear, and feel the effects of the passage of time, the loss of so much (even as we gain), the inevitable cycle of growth and decay. Where is our security? What can we hold on to?

Hemingway's "lost generation" suffered from a loss of faith. The famous French philosopher Jean-Paul Sartre felt existential nausea in the face of nothingness. Kerouac's beat generation sought detachment and spiritual transcendence from bland conformity through individuality in creative lifestyles. The sixties generation rebelled against convention to find freedom for themselves and for others. Some of today's generation of youth see a bitter, hostile world around them. But if we suspend our belief in any and every world view, we are left in the midst of emptiness!

Emptiness leads into suffering, and emptiness also shows the way out of suffering. When we embrace emptiness, without clinging or yearning for something beyond it, transcendence becomes possible.

Wisdom Is Found by Entering the Void

The feared empty space is a fertile void. Exploring it
is a turning point towards therapeutic change.
—Wilson Van Dusen in Stevens, 1975, 90

An unexamined life leads to suffering, as the Four Noble Truths have shown. Ordinary living can distract us from exploring more deeply, and there is a price to pay if we become out of touch—when circumstances push and pull, you are not in the driver's seat. To recognize your true nature takes awareness.

Inner change often begins by being willing to enter the void. You can stay with emptiness and trust that there you will find new freedom and new solutions. So no matter what difficulty you are confronting, no matter how challenging it may seem, you may find a new alternative in emptiness.

When people have difficulties, they often avoid noticing. They look away, forming gaps in perception and awareness. By facing the gaps, people often feel like they are facing an intimidating nothingness, like falling down a deep, dark hole. But if you have faith in emptiness, you become aware. And with that awareness, you discover enlightenment to light your way, guiding you through the darkness.

Facing the Void with Meditation

Emptiness is the deeper nature of all things. The meditations here will help you to develop skills for recognizing and staying with emptiness. You will come to an understanding of emptiness through your meditation. These exercises are like a boat that carries you across the river—once you get to the other shore, step out and explore the territory. Your own consciousness is the fertile ground for discovery. Have confidence in yourself and your capacities as they develop.

Meditation can bring inner calm and a sense of tranquility. It's not something you try to bring about; it just happens of itself. Inner calm is the environment of emptiness, an unobstructed pathway to wisdom.

Tranquility arises from emptiness. With the experience of emptiness, nothing is there to get in the way, yet everything is possible in the infinite void. So there is a freedom from the known, with just as much potential for the uncreated as the created. You need not be held back by what has been, because all things change and evolve.

People sometimes worry that tranquility will be boring. But a tranquil mind is not a motionless mind. Rather, it means being free from obstructions, unhampered by inner pressures. The tranquil mind can be active or quiet—whatever is needed to meet life fully and dynamically. A tranquil mind from meditation is imperturbable, steady, composed, and in control.

If you want to invite a tranquil mind and heart, meditate. Don't put the cart before the horse: just meditate daily and tranquility develops. Meditate deeply. Find your way into meditation by starting with wherever you are. If you are feeling nothing, even if you are tempted to ignore it, use this experience as an opportunity to face the void. As you begin to meditate, let yourself feel the nothingness. Keep meditating on your experiencing as it evolves. You may begin to feel the glimmer of something, perhaps sadness or frustration. Trust yourself in each moment. You are okay as you stay with the present moment and keep focused. Explore the emptiness and stay attuned to it, and you will deepen your understanding of yourself. Relax with the experience. Don't try, just do.

Meditative Calm

Sit quietly in meditation. Recall a relaxing place, such as a beautiful ocean, a peaceful forest, or a meandering stream. It could be somewhere you have visited or an imagined place. Visualize it as clearly as you can. The silence is profound. This moment is absolute stillness. Imagine that you are there. Allow your thoughts, breathing, and muscles to settle down as you enjoy being there. Be a part of this scene and allow yourself to become completely still, without effort.

Emptiness Meditation

Sit down for meditation. Close your eyes, or keep them half open, and use one of the Clearing the Mind meditations in lesson 4. When you feel quiet and calm, let go and just sit in emptiness. Don't follow any images or thoughts that intrude. Allow yourself to experience deeply without conceptualizing in any way. With nothing in mind: no fear, no disgust, no pleasure, no pain, just be fully present in the moment, in the absolute Now, "Empty and marvelous," in the words of Zen master Ma-tzu.

Meditate regularly to discover your source for inner calm and confidence. Emptiness is a resource that can always be there for you. The potential from the empty center is infinite.

Mind Is All There Is

We think this is real
That's what it seems
But what we perceive
Is only a dream.
This and that
Are mere selections
Illusions of objects
From mind's reflections
So let empty space
Be in your mind
Then Nirvana's clear light
Will peacefully shine
—C. Alexander Simpkins

Natural Attitude versus Mind Only

People usually believe in the reality of things. We take for granted that the world we perceive is here today. We also assume that the same world will be here tomorrow. The problem is that sometimes these taken-for-granted views of the world hold us back. They become barriers to new and creative possibilities. When you can free your mind of limitations, you will find it easier to realize your hopes and dreams.

Science extends this natural attitude by assuming that we can observe and measure because the world does exist and is real. From this perspective, we can build our understanding with improved methods of measurement and more sensitive instruments.

Buddhism takes a radically different attitude, a deconstructionist view that leads to Nirvana. We shouldn't be so certain about existence; we can't really say yes or no. We make an error if we naively assume that the world as we perceive it really exists.

We can perform tests to check out the reality of a given state of affairs. If an object as perceived is really there, we should be able to test its physical attributes. For example, we could weigh it, lift it up and down to feel its weight, compare it to another object of similar weight, or contrast it with an object of a different weight. We could submerge it in water and measure how much water is displaced. But all these tests don't necessarily prove the constant reality of the object. They simply give us information about the temporary reality of the object as it appears at that moment. Our tests confirm an object we believe in is partly a result of perception.

Beyond Appearances to Emptiness

We have no direct proof, without any doubt, that the object we measure today is identical to the object we measure tomorrow.

Time, by a succession of instances, gives us the convincing illusion of continuous existence, and as a result, we create the perceived world with our consciousness.

The objects of our mind appear fixed, permanent, and lasting. But can you look beyond the appearances to the deeper, transitory, empty nature? Take a particular example, such as the emotion you feel toward someone. Look beyond the various moods you have. Consider how this person is changing, day by day. Look back over years and ahead to the future. Try to grasp a deeper sense of that person, beyond your opinions and concepts of him or her.

Mind Creates the Illusions

But then why does this perceived world seem so real? Driving down the road on a hot, sunny day, looking ahead at the highway in the distance, we may see a pool of water reflecting the hot sun: a mirage. The mirage seems very real, but seeming doesn't make it so.

The illusion of a constant object is partly created by our consciousness filling in the gaps. When we listen to a series of varying tones over a stable period of time, our mind flows the notes together. We hear music. Watching a series of pictures varying slightly or even greatly, if presented correctly, flickering at a certain range or speed, we see moving scenes: a movie. Our minds put the separate pictures together to give us a unity, and its reality is experienced by us as constant. The movie looks like a continuous flow of appearances to which we respond. This is our consciousness constructing existence.

Here is another example of how the solid, real quality of the world is actually mental constructs. If you showed a CD to someone from a nontechnological society, they might notice the round, flat shape and rainbowlike reflection from the recorded side, but they won't know what it really is or does. Without conceptual understanding, the CD as CD would not really exist for that primitive individual.

How Concepts Add the Illusion of Permanence

We are also deceived into thinking that what we experience is permanent from the names and labels we give things. For example, we label the large shading plant outside as an oak tree. We recognize the tree as the same oak tree whenever we see it. But this label is really an arbitrary convention, sustained by the mind. It is an abstraction from the real, growing life form that changes from season to season, day to day, minute to minute. We come to experience the tree as our abstract label—oak tree—and think of it as solid and lasting. But in five hundred years, the tree will be gone. If you have ever seen a time-lapse film of a flower opening and then closing again, you have had a glimpse into the ever-present change process, which is usually taking place too slowly to notice. The duration of things varies, but everything is in transition.

Western Illustrations of Mind-Only

Buddhist theories about how we construct reality are not foreign to Western thought. Several pivotal philosophers have discussed similar ideas. John Locke (1632–1704) was one of the foremost Western philosophers. His concepts had a profound influence on the American political system. He asked himself where all the ideas in our mind come from. His answer was, "From Experience. In that, all our Knowledge is founded, and from that it ultimately derives itself" (Locke, 1690/1975, 104).

Locke performed an interesting experiment to show how our experience influences our ideas about the world. He filled three buckets with water: one hot, one cold, and one lukewarm. He held one hand in the hot bucket and the other in the cold bucket for a few minutes. Then he immediately placed both hands into the lukewarm bucket. To the hand that had been in the hot bucket, the water felt cold, and to the hand that had been in the cold bucket, the water felt warm. But how could the same water feel as if it is two different temperatures? Locke explained this paradox by pointing out that the world we experience is created by our sensations and mental reflections upon our sensations.

George Berkeley (1685–1753), a renowned philosopher and Catholic bishop, took Locke's ideas one step further. He sounded much like a Buddhist when he stated that the world we experience does not exist without the mind to perceive it:

> All the choir of heaven and furniture of the earth, in a word all these bodies which compose the mighty frame of the world, have not any substance without a mind, that their being is to be perceived or known (Berkeley, 1820, Vol. 1, 27).

The Buddha understood this insight long before Bishop Berkeley: "All that we are is the result of what we have thought: It is founded on our thoughts, it is made up of our thoughts" (*Dhammapada* in Yutang 1942, 327). He believed this insight was liberating. If our minds create our world of suffering, then our minds can also free us from suffering in it.

Deconstructing Reality Contemplation
Think about a movie you have seen. Recall the story, the scenes, and how it all looks very real, even though you know the characters are just actors on the screen. Now take another step away and think about the person behind the projector who makes it happen. He can stop the projector and the movie vanishes, or start it again and the illusion of the movie reappears. Can you relate this to the reality sense you have?

Activities of the Mind
The reality that we know and experience is created by the mind. A disturbed mind creates disturbance around it. Enlightened consciousness can see through illusion to become free from the bonds of limited biases. A calm, enlightened mind creates a calm, enlightened world.

Suchness
In lesson 6 we explored the dependent co-origination of the world, how all things come into existence together in a single moment. In that moment when things appear in the world, they appear in a certain way, as they are. This is their suchness. The true nature of the world is its suchness, and the true nature of suchness is empty. We add explanations, concepts, and hierarchies, but the true nature of things is without these characteristics.

Suchness—as it is—is individuality devoid of a self nature. The center of the manifest world is the relationship between its elements. Then our world of meaning must also be related to the objects, events, and people we interact with. But these objects, people, and events have no independent existence outside of their relationship. They exist for a flash, a moment of time, then are gone. But that moment of time is significant and real, just not lasting independently. Like a cloud of particles in a cloudy wave, our world of relationships comes into being and then goes out of being. We cannot stop time and we don't need to.

Suchness in its emptiness is releasing and reassuring. You set rigid concepts aside, and suffering disappears. There is no craving, since all is ultimately empty of permanent substance and existence. What is there to crave? All is transitory, temporary, a mental construction. So although suffering must be accepted for what it is, for now, it is time limited. Suffering is not independent of circumstance and time.

Meditation can free us from our mental constructions, bringing us back to emptiness, to the suchness of reality, which means such as it really is.

Beyond Concepts Meditation

Sit in meditation and close your eyes. Attend fully and completely to each moment as you experience it. Pay attention to the details without forming a concept about the experience. If you are feeling warmth, don't label it, just feel the sensation. If you are trying to hold on to it or express it in a concept or thought, you are moving away from the reality of the warmth itself. Just feel, see, and hear the experience, whatever it is, as it is, moment to moment, without comparison or contrast. Let it be such as it is.

Meditation on Everything, Just as It Is

Sit in meditation and be fully present without thought. Experience yourself and your surroundings as you sit. Can you be fully present without any other mental comments or assessments, just present, relaxed, and at ease? You don't have to do anything or go anywhere, just be here now. Feel the peaceful moment. Everything is okay.

Effective Problem Solving

The ideas presented in this lesson can free your thinking to be open and flexible, ready to solve problems. When we are confronted with a problem, we tend to look for a solution that fits the definition we give to the problem. But sometimes the definitions the mind creates are too narrow and limited. Effective problem solving begins by opening your mind with meditation.

Opening Options Meditation

Meditate for several minutes, clearing your mind. Then describe a problem as it seems, in exact detail, without evaluating it. For example, perhaps you are having a problem completing a project. Do not condemn or justify it by saying it's unfair that you have this problem.

Don't attempt to solve the problem until you have carefully defined what it is. Maybe you think the problem is that you don't have enough time to get the job done or that other people are preventing you from solving it. Try to broaden your definition or propose an alternative definition of the problem. Next think of the opposite: you are not having a problem completing the project or that you have already completed it successfully. Do you get any new ideas about your problem?

Deconstructing Problems

Things are not what they seem. Nothing exists as it appears. All is transitory. Apply this perspective to your problem. Sometimes the problem may seem overwhelming. But this may be just a daunting illusion, a construct of the mind. The actual problem is just what it is. So deconstruct, and try to face the real problem just as it is, as you go along. Try applying one of the basic themes, such as the transitory nature of reality, as a tool.

How is your problem transitory? From the transitory perspective, in the above example the project is time limited. It will pass. You will probably do the job and then it will be over. Then you go on to the next project. Or perhaps you are creating a rigid, fixed concept about time. Challenge and then let go of your inflexible concepts. Focus your full attention on the work so that all that really exists is each moment. Then the task will be completed one step at a time. This is just one example. Try to recognize how many problems are constructed by your mind.

Meditative Moment on Your Problem

Close your eyes and meditate for a few minutes. Get in touch with the problem in this very moment. Don't jump ahead to what is due tomorrow or how much you did or did not accomplish yesterday. Just be in the moment. With meditative awareness, approach your problem and you will accomplish it well.

Understanding Mind Only can free you from the constraints of your self-created limitations. Return to your immediate experiencing by meditating. In time, barriers dissolve and impossible situations don't seem quite so hopeless. You discover new solutions and alternative paths. The way is cleared and the vista of potential is open before you.

Art

Creating Outside the Box

. . . to forget the object, yes to forget it—to put it out of
our minds entirely and think only of planes, lines, colours,
rhythms, etc. emotional visual quality . . .
> —Morgan Russell, American artist in Paris 1912 in
> The Tate Gallery 1980, 210

Buddhism's perspective is useful for creative minds. Concepts of
objects usually point us away from their deeper nature. Freedom
from fixed concepts of objects leads us to deconstruct reality,
including time and space as we know it. For artists, this can be
liberating, permitting new and more open and experimental
forms and themes to emerge for creative expression. No object
has to be present for art to point to and express something tangible and meaningful. Therefore abstractions of lines or color
without an object become a more real and complete way to
point to true nature.

In the Black Square (Im schwarzen Viereck), Wassily Kandinsky. June 1923. Oil on canvas. Solomon R. Guggenheim Museum, New York. Gift, Solomon R. Guggenheim, 1937. 37. 254.

Wassily Kandinsky (1866–1944), foremost theoretician and dean of abstract art at the famous Bauhaus school in Germany (1919–1933), encouraged artists to attune to and express the spiritual roots of art itself. He believed that resonance with the spectator's own spirit would then be possible. Buddhism harmonizes perfectly with this frame of reference.

Direct and Indirect: Art Expresses Buddhism

Art can express and harmonize with Buddhist themes, both directly and indirectly. The figures and stories of Buddhism are depicted directly within drawings, paintings, sculptures, and architecture. These themes are also represented indirectly in art, as space, form, and pattern become ways to express the deeper sense of Buddhism's meanings.

Direct Art

Most people are familiar with direct expressions of Buddhist art. As a direct representation of Buddhist principles, Buddhist art includes paintings, sculptures, writings, and architecture of Buddhist figures and themes to inspire and instruct. Specific gestures, postures, and theories are also traditionally depicted.

Paintings, sculptures, and images of Buddha created over many centuries are the most prevalent forms of Buddhist art. Often seen seated in meditation, Buddha is a timeless image. These pieces of art reveal Buddha's meditative state of absolute calm and serenity. Statues of Buddha have played a significant role in history. They were given as gifts from one country to another to transmit the spirit of Buddhism. The first such transmission came from India to China.

Seated Bodhisattva, artist unknown. Sui dynasty (581–618), Chinese. Stone with polychrome. Bequest of Mrs. Cora Timken Burnett, San Diego Museum of Art.

The way Buddha is portrayed conveys the deeper understandings of Buddhism. In early sculptures, Buddha sat in a meditation posture. Later sculptures added decorations and adornments as the idea of Buddha shifted from the early Hinayana vision of a noble person who found enlightenment, to the Mahayana conception of Buddha as a universal spiritual presence. Paintings of Buddha also reflected the shift; early paintings showed Buddha in natural settings as a real person, and later ones showed him at the center of elaborate landscapes in the company of many followers.

Tibetan artists evolved the *mandala* as an art form that is appreciated around the world. Mandalas are circular, with layers of circles expanding outward. Geometric shapes sometimes represent the four directions. One type of mandala depicts Buddha in the center, surrounded by his disciples and his temples. Some mandalas symbolize the entire universe as it appears in a single moment of suchness. Symbolism is used in mandalas to communicate layers of meaning, from the outer appearance of the varied world to the depths of enlightened consciousness. Practitioners use mandalas for meditation, to help point awareness toward deeper consciousness.

Zen artists used *sumi-e* ink paintings to create direct scenes of Buddha, Buddhist patriarchs, and historical scenes or stories about anonymous monks. Each painting shows a person performing everyday activities such as walking, crossing a river on a boat, or meditating. These works illustrate the Zen idea that enlightenment is here and now, part of daily life, when walking, eating, and sleeping—nothing special. This sensitive art form gives a direct experience of Buddhism to the viewer. A few black brush strokes against a vast white background suggest emptiness and serenity.

Form Is Emptiness: Indirect Art

Rocks, gardens, water, birds and other items in nature are some typical subjects used for indirect Buddhist art. Fine arts are extended to other mediums such as the strange music of the Shakuhachi flute. Indirectly, Buddhist ideas have been adapted for inspiration and justification of abstraction and pattern. Even imperfections in material expression or substance can be used to express Buddhist themes.

Buddhist art speaks for itself, as it is—not because it was done by a famous artist, but because of what the art piece expresses. The inner core of Buddhist art is its suchness, not just its personal meaning. Soetsu Yanagi, the founder of the folk crafts revival movement in Japan, greatly revered plain, primitive, unsigned Korean pottery because it represented the unadorned quality of an enlightened mind. Art from simple, primitive sources is beautiful and true to the essence. Art may be found everywhere, even in unexpected places.

Emptiness, the deeper nature of reality in Buddhism, is frequently expressed in abstract art. Asymmetrical paintings led artists to create simple, almost barren works that express emptiness. As an interconnected unity, dependent co-origination can be expressed in pattern. So, an object or its lack can both be expressive of Buddhism's doctrines. And there are many other ways to utilize these principles creatively. As Marshall McLuhan said prophetically in the 1960s, the "medium is the message."

Objects are not just physical objects: they can be used to display the true nature of reality through the mind of the artist and the beholder. A rock then becomes an aesthetic object of consciousness. First the object is seen in its suchness, interconnected to the Oneness. Meaning or interpretation is secondary. But as you look more carefully at, for example, a lonely rock in the middle of a Zen garden, you can feel the emptiness there too.

The art of Bonseki uses rocks and pebbles to create beautiful scenes. Masters of this art collect rocks and gravel of various sizes, shapes, and sorts for use in creating landscapes, pictures, and even gardens. Seascapes are dry with pebbles and rocks of various sizes for effect, yet they can have a very fluid appearance.

Some contemporary Asian modern artists, known as Sho, paint using the calligraphic gesture and line as principle for technique. They have extended calligraphy into areas previously unexplored by classical artists. These artists elegantly paint brush strokes, which may depict a figure or a landscape in black ink. The open space of the canvas becomes part of the artistic work. Movement and rhythm give dynamic vitality to the work. The artist makes creative links through analogies with music, dance, and poetry. No distinctions need to be made, in keeping with the Buddhist principle of nonduality and interdependence, so a Buddhist-inspired painting has rhythm and tone like a musical piece, and may express words or images as part of it.

Artists often use their personal truths and interests as the central themes of their art pieces. Your own personal truth and interests in Buddhism make excellent sources for themes and subjects of artistic expressions.

Sensing Form and Emptiness
Find a simple but creatively inspiring ordinary object such as a rock or stone. Gather several of these rocks together and place them down in front of you. Then close your eyes and pick up one of the rocks without looking. Notice the texture, temperature,

Bursts of Insight, Carmen Z. Simpkins. 1971, United States. Acrylic on paper.

and weight. Can you feel the rock without definition, just as it is? Open your eyes and look at the rock. Try to perceive it out of context, without interpretation, as both form and emptiness. You may substitute any other natural object you would like.

Emptiness Is Form

If form is emptiness, as in the *Heart Sutra*, then artists can express emptiness through form. Abstract artists created without an object in mind, without an intended meaning except the one emerging in the moment of creation itself. Meaning evolves in the act of creating. The abstract artists are in a very real sense pointing to emptiness. You can use their art to experience the emptiness behind objects, events, and also sounds.

Forms are shown in vacuous ways, with as little definition as possible, to permit the inner emptiness to shine forth. A face is just as it is, its lines, its colors. The definition comes from comprehension of the whole, and subsequently, an attempt to communicate about the unity.

When the context is removed, perception changes. Color, form, and pattern can give an experience of emptiness.

Viewing Four Ways

Step outside the form by experimenting with the *Bursts of Insight* painting on the previous page. Look at the painting and see whatever forms and patterns are there for you. Try turning it upside down. What do you see now? View the painting from various angles to comprehend it in many ways. Notice how you can see different images each way you hold the painting.

Now try to look at it as simply tone and pattern. Try to let go of any objective interpretation and feel your reaction.

Abstract Emptiness Is Form

Emptiness is the inner nature of all things, but we often overlook it. This exercise may help you to break through stereotypical perception.

Take an abstract walk around a park or your own backyard. Try to see each possible abstract category as emptiness. So instead of saying form is emptiness, emptiness is form, notice the color of the ground and say, "Color is emptiness and emptiness is color." Or "This square shape is emptiness and emptiness is this square shape." Consider the meaning of what you are saying on a deep level. Without the abstract parts, no whole is possible. But the whole is always more than just its parts. Or is it?

Emptiness in Action

Abstract art, performance art, and music all permit contemplation with prajnaparamita consciousness. A gesture by a dancer, the burning of a canvas with a blowtorch, atonal sounds of music all partake of the notion that form of any kind is symbolic, showing us that form is emptiness and emptiness is form. The following artists are just a few examples among many who broke through barriers of form to find and creatively express the formless.

Jackson Pollock (1912–1956)

From the perspective of Buddhism, action is empty, so action paintings in which action is used to create a painting, such as the works of Jackson Pollock, can give an experience of emptiness through the action itself. Action gives energy and non-objectively points to the ever-present relationship between emptiness and form.

Pollock created dynamic abstract paintings with splashes of color at a high intensity. Pollock's painting style—using powerful, flowing action by the artist to apply paint—inspired many variations by other abstract artists. His method of deep, personal involvement, often walking about or even riding a bicycle on a large canvas, dripping and swirling paint from brushes and containers, can be understood as another form of detachment, through complete, concentrated immersion in the process of

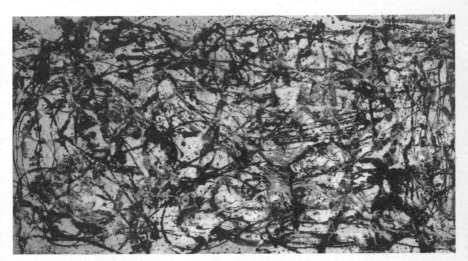

Enchanted Forest, Jackson Pollock. 1947. Oil on canvas. The Solomon R. Guggenheim Foundation, New York. Peggy Guggenheim Collection, Venice, 1976. 76. 2553. 151.

creation to the point of losing himself. Boundaries can temporarily dissolve when art is used in this way. No boundaries remain between actions for expression of creative imagery and action.

Yves Klein (1928–1962)

Another abstract artist, Yves Klein, developed his own brand of what has come to be called performance art. Klein had a brief life, but in a manner similar to Van Gogh, his intense artistic work expressed creative themes that we still see today in modern art. He invented and patented a unique ultramarine blue color in a clear medium, called international Klein blue. Deep shades of blue are often used for mysterious and unusual effects in many kinds of artistic productions.

Klein's work took on a nonobjective meaning in performances, which he created in front of an audience or alone in his own studio. Klein also sometimes burned paintings with a blowtorch, leaving the creative marks of fire's dynamic energy.

Twentieth-century abstract artists used another central theme from Buddhism, nonattachment, as an attitude to inspire great works of creativity. One example is Klein's human brushes. He evolved his individualistic techniques for creating paintings by applying paint to the bodies of artist's models and then verbally directing them as human brushes to walk over and impress the paint on large canvases. By this means he intended to keep himself as the artist detached while creating. Sometimes he involved his spectators in the creation as participants, experimenting with ways of creating that stretched or extended the boundaries of nonattachment far beyond objective representation.

Blue Sponge (L'Eponge bleue), Yves Klein. 1959. Dry pigment in synthetic
resin on sponge with metal rod and stone base. Solomon R.
Guggenheim Museum, New York. Gift, Mrs. Andrew P. Fuller, 1964.
64. 1752. Photograph by David Heald © SRGF, NY.

Art   **115**

Nonattachment continues to inspire artists in the twenty-first century. As technology evolves and the medium of expression in art becomes more complex, artists contribute their artistic vision without attachment to the past, allowing them to move boldly forward.

John Cage (1912–1992)

Formless form was also expressed in twentieth century music. John Cage, a famous abstract musician, studied Zen Buddhism under D.T. Suzuki. He artistically explored the nature of music itself, using sounds and silence and audience experiences to synthesize a unique tapestry of music. He believed the definition of what we think of as music was too narrow. He decided to include noise and silence as valuable parts of musical expression, to show that there are no walls between art and life: Samsara is Nirvana.

Cage preferred to create with random events and to bring the audience sounds into his music. In one of his most renowned concerts, Cage walked out onto the stage, sat down ceremoniously at a grand piano, opened the piano, and then did nothing for a fixed period of time. The concert consisted of silence along with subtle sounds from the audience: breathing, coughing, and movement of chairs and clothing. As the concert progressed, the audience gradually came to recognize that they were part of an artist production that was taking place. Cage presented his audience with an empty moment and showed that music is everywhere, in everything, and also in nothing. You can apply this insight to other contexts.

These artists are a few examples among many who broke through barriers of form to find and creatively express the formless. If you would like to experience firsthand the effects of non-representational, nonobjective art, go to a museum, take some books out of the library, or look online at the Websites about abstract modern art, such as on Klein, Pollock, Cage, and others. The Website for the Guggenheim Museum, located in New York City, is also devoted to abstract art in detail. View these experiences from a Buddhist perspective, and new possibilities will present themselves to you.

Freeing Your Creative Process

The creative process is an expression outside the boundaries of the known, the freedom to step away from what has been done before. You can use your Buddhist understandings to navigate the uncharted waters of creativity.

Going Beyond Concepts

Concepts may hold you back from creating something new, so use your meditative skills to take you beyond the conceptual level. For example, if you are painting a landscape of a tree on a hill with blue sky, try setting aside the labels: tree, hill, sky. Instead, clear your mind as you observe the scene. Notice the colors, the patterns, the lines or whatever else you see or feel in the momentary meditative experience.

Use meditation for any artistic medium. Let go of melody and notes to hear rhythms, tones, and frequencies for new forms of music to emerge. Move beyond preset positions or steps to create new dance movements.

Meditate deeply on emptiness and then let yourself create. We wonder what unique works you will discover!

Flowers Break Out of Their Shell, Naomi Minkin. 1965,
United States. Egg shell mosaic. Private collection.

Creating Something from Nothing

Emptiness is the fertile void of possibility. One artist from our
family, Naomi Minkin (1926–1979), characterized her art as
creating something from nothing. She combined many different
media such as painting, sewing, and sculpture into her creations.
One of her unusual works was a large, soft sculpture created
with fabric and foam. Minkin used everyday objects artistically.
She made a decorative pillowcase into a dress. A coke can
became a sculpture. Broken dishes or eggshells were made into

a mosaic. If you let go of typical definitions of materials and methods, new possibilities emerge.

From Nothing to Something
Make some random marks on a blank page, such as lines and shapes leaving large spaces in between. Then creatively make them into a drawing. You can also share the experience with a friend, passing the drawing back and forth for other possible creations. Vary this exercise by putting together groups of small objects such as sticks, wire, wood, or colored paper. Think outside the box!

Meditation from Nothing to Something
Meditate for several minutes. Use one of the clearing-the-mind meditations from lesson 4. Let go of concepts of function and use by staying in the present moment. Remember Nagarjuna's argument in lesson one that nothing has an inherent function for all time. Immediately following meditation, let your imagination come up with possible everyday objects to be used as the materials for your creation. Without boundaries of what a thing is or is not to hold you back, anything is possible.

Creative Interdependence and Oneness
Your creativity can be enhanced by meditating on Oneness. Another accomplished artist from our family, Carmen Simpkins (1913–) is an abstract painter who also plays the violin. When asked about her art, she says that she considers herself a musician whose instrument is the paintbrush. She paints to music, forgetting herself as the sounds inspire movements of the brush, colors, and patterns. An unplanned original painting emerges,

surprising even her. Sometimes, looking at it later, she may not even remember painting it. The painting seemed to just happen.

Meditation on Creative Interdependence
Meditate on Oneness. Let yourself feel how everything is interrelated to everything else. For example, mindfully follow your breathing, in and out. As you observe the process, carefully pay attention to the feeling: How the air you breathe comes in from the outer environment, and then through the actions of respiration, becomes part of you. The exact boundary is uncertain. Think of other ways that you are One with everything else.

Allow yourself to feel the interrelation of all artistic mediums: music, painting, sculpture, drama, and dance. You will make your own discoveries as the experience of Oneness becomes more vivid for you.

The openness of creating can be extended into everyday living. The years and events of your life are like the canvas and paints of the painter, to be formed in patterns as you create your life and are created by it. As you take a creative, open perspective, you can travel on a pathway to enlightenment. When you try to approach your life creatively, you may discover that you don't need or want old, taken-for-granted obstacles you had adapted to. Lesson 9 will show you how to overcome barriers that might seem to block the way.

Lesson
Nine
_____

Overcoming Obstacles to an Enlightened Life

"All the evil deeds I have committed in the past are due to greed, anger, and folly cherished since the time beyond calculation,
And have been produced by means of my body, mouth, and mind—
All these I now confess without reservation."
—Self-Reflective Vow of Buddhist Monks in
Suzuki 1994, 73

We are all born with the capacity for enlightened living, but we often let our own shortcomings get in the way. Remove the obstacles and a spiritually enlightened life opens up. Obstructions dissolve, revealing what is naturally within, a pure and clear Buddha nature.

When people join a Buddhist monastery to become monks, they undergo a rigorous process to train the mind, body, and

Sri Yantra, a focus for meditation. C. Alexander Simpkins Jr. 2003.

spirit. Ta-hui, a famous Zen Buddhist monk from the Sung period in China, called upon his students to face the challenges so that they could transcend their problems and discover the wisdom of Nirvana. May his words inspire you in your own journey:

> If you want to know who this one is, dive down into
> the depths of your being where no intellection is possible
> to reach; and when you know it, you know that there
> is a place where neither birth nor death can touch (Suzuki
> 1994, 7).

The problems of life are created by the mind. You can overcome your difficulties by making changes in your mental processes. Through self-analysis and meditation, you undergo a transformation that will help you take control of your destiny and open your life to Nirvana. This lesson helps you deal with common obstructions to the pure, enlightened wisdom that lies dormant, waiting to be discovered.

Seeking Assistance When Needed

If you find that you cannot get past your obstacles, even after making a sincere effort, we encourage you to consult a Buddhist Center. There are many different kinds of Buddhist organizations located in most large cities, with warm and friendly people who are ready to help.

Some people may be more comfortable with conventional psychotherapy. And some problems might be more directly addressed with the support of a therapeutic relationship. If you choose this path, try to find a therapist who is sympathetic with Eastern philosophy. Then your psychotherapeutic process

works in synchrony with Buddhism. Eastern and Western healing can go hand in hand, as cross-cultural approaches become
more mainstream.

Start Small

In the silence
Between the spaces
We can hear
The Voice of thoughts
So Clear
——C. Alexander Simpkins

Have you ever become annoyed with another driver on the
road? Have you found yourself feeling irritated when someone
was rude to you at a store? Do you continue to ruminate about
small grievances for hours after, feeling ill-tempered and
unhappy? If you ever let life's small frustrations get to you, you
have an opportunity to explore and grow. The famous hyp-
notherapist Milton H. Erickson believed that when people make
even one small change, they set a process of transformation into
motion.

Empty Self, Empty Other

Don't fill in meanings for what the person who annoys you is
doing or intending. When a salesman treats you rudely or
another driver cuts in front of you, let go of your interpretations
that they are trying to put you down, shame you, or deliberately
anger you. Leave space for the unknown. By making nothing of
it and allowing the situation to empty of any interpretation, you
react to it just as it is: small and insignificant.

Mindful Awareness

Following coping with a minor annoyance, let it go and then move on, paying close attention to each moment. For example, if you are in a store, keep being aware as you walk away from the counter, as you walk outside the store, as you move on to the next errand. Notice only what is happening in each moment. Don't replay the previous disturbance in your mind. That moment has passed and you are on to another, filled with potential for new and more positive interactions.

Try to consider the rude salesman or driver with compassion. Perhaps something negative is happening in his or her life to lead to such an inconsiderate action. But do not bring the negative into your own life. Can you feel compassion for the other person's suffering?

Working with Moods

Small things can build up and lead to chronic moodiness, which is an obstacle to a spiritually enlightened life. However, you can become steadier and calmer. If you are troubled by chronic anger, irritability, or depressed moods, begin the change process by meditating regularly. Use the meditations from this book. Begin with several minutes a day, working up to thirty minutes. Regular meditation practice can become a resource for calm and stability in your life.

Get in Touch Mindfully and Embrace Suffering

If you feel a negative mood coming on, turn your attention to it mindfully. Notice your body sensations, your emotions, your thoughts, and any outer circumstances that are happening. Stay in touch with each moment as it unfolds. Don't add anything that is not there, just observe each feeling and thought without getting carried away on a tangent. Stay with the mood, even if it is uncomfortable. Accept it for what it is, without adding to it. This is what you are feeling right now. But it will pass, especially if you can view it within a broader context of meaning. Consider your situation from the perspective of impermanence: This feeling will also inevitably alter over time. Perhaps you cannot see past it at this moment, but think back on a similar time and remember how the feeling eventually passed. Trust the inevitable flow of time and wait patiently. If you can, inwardly challenge your attitude about the situation.

Using the Eightfold Path to Transform Your Moods: Right Views

Apply the Four Noble Truths and the Eightfold Path. Look at your circumstance and consider your beliefs or assumptions. The mood you feel is intimately connected to what you think about your circumstance, other people, and your life in general.

Analyze your views using the Eightfold Path: Do you believe that life should always satisfy your own personal ego, to be just how you want it to be? If things don't live up to your expectations, do you feel let down, angry, irritable, or depressed? Perhaps you are taking Wrong Views such as clinging to unreasonable wishes for personal pleasures or trying to satisfy a need due to a rigid self-concept. Notice your views, intent, speech, and actions.

Right Effort

Mobilize your Right Effort. You may not feel like trying hard when you are in a negative mood, but keep focused on your greater commitment to living an aware, enlightened life. If you have been meditating regularly, you will find it easier to apply the Eightfold Path under challenging circumstances. If you are unable to do it while under duress, wait, and meditate more often. Then try again the next time you feel moody. Be patient, and keep trying. It should get easier over time.

Deconstructing Moods

Think about how your patterns of thought might be creating your mood. Trace back to when you first started feeling this most recent mood and try to remember what came right before. Like a detective, you can discover clues to help you figure out how you are construing situations to bring about unwholesome thoughts. Are you making negative judgments about yourself or others? Or are you engaging in unwholesome patterns of thought such as greed, hatred, or excessive pride?

When you have recognized and challenged your unwholesome thinking, substitute wholesome thoughts. Think about the Buddha, Nirvana, emptiness, and your positive potential for change.

Calming and Clearing

If you find it difficult to calm down, put yourself into a calming situation, such as your quiet meditation room (or corner) with subdued lighting, incense burning, and soft meditation music playing.

Sit in meditation. Pay close attention to your breathing and allow it to become calm. Let your muscles relax as much as you can. As you sit quietly, encourage your body to become more relaxed and comfortable. Relax very deeply, just sitting.

Overcoming Anxiety

Fritz Perls, the founder of Gestalt Therapy, said, "Anxiety is the gap between the now and the then." (Perls 1969, 3) He believed that when people leave their moment-to-moment experiencing, they block the natural flow of ongoing spontaneous energy, leading to a feeling of anxiety. By returning to the absolute now—the present moment—energy can flow naturally into activity, and anxiety diminishes. Learning how to return to the present, the absolute now, helps resolve anxiety.

Here and Now

This mindfulness exercise is also used in Gestalt Therapy. Mindful awareness can help you develop a calm, attuned meditative presence.

Sit down somewhere where you won't be disturbed. Make descriptive statements of details you observe, either aloud or to yourself, beginning each one with "Now I am aware that . . ." or Here I am aware of . . ." Keep following the flow of your awareness in the present moment. If you find yourself leaving the present to remember something or think about the future say, "Now I am aware that I am thinking about the past (or the future). Now I realize this. Now I return my focus to the present. Now I feel comfortable again." Keep your reference in the present moment.

Meditation to Let Go of Distinctions

Anxiety also comes about when people make distinctions, comparisons, and self-evaluations. Through meditation, you can learn to walk the middle path between yes and no, better and worse, to simply be fully who and what you are.

Meditate on your present experiencing without making any evaluations or comparisons. So for example, if you find yourself thinking, "I feel better than yesterday," or "I can't focus today," bring yourself back to the present moment of just sitting. Sense what is there without adding to it or interpreting or thinking anything about it. As soon as you notice yourself making an evaluation, bring yourself back to the present experience. This meditation becomes easier with practice. Gradually you will feel some calming and relaxing of your anxiety.

Anxiety as Blocked Energy

When people experience anxiety, they often feel it physically as tightness in their chest or abdominal area. Generalized muscle tension may also be present. Becoming aware of your breathing can help to release unnecessary tensions and relieve anxiety.

Breathing Meditation to Ease Anxiety

Lie down on your back and raise your knees so that your feet rest flat on the floor. Close your eyes and then turn your attention to your breathing. Mindfully listen to the sound as the air goes in through your nose and down into your lungs. Allow your ribcage and chest to expand and then return to rest as you exhale. Let breathing be natural and relaxed, without forcing. Keep listening to the sound of your breathing, in and out, until you feel ready to stop. You will feel more relaxed and less anxious.

Anxiety as a Sign

Buddhism teaches that your own mind is the pathway to deeper understanding. As you become more mindful of what you are experiencing, you can be in touch with what is needed.

Mindful Meditation: Listening to Yourself

Next time you feel anxious, pay close attention to your thoughts. Notice if you seem to be imaginatively talking to someone in your mind, perhaps someone you need to work things out with. Or perhaps you are going over concerns about some task you have been avoiding. Become aware of your own inner dialogue and listen! With mindful attention and an open, tolerant attitude, you may discover what you really need to take care of or come to terms with. Your anxiety may be indirectly trying to tell you something important.

Moderating Impulses

Many people are bothered by cravings and impulses that they cannot control. When you are troubled by habits you would like to change such as smoking, overeating, or drinking, finding the Middle Way can help you put an end to your cravings and discover inner fulfillment.

The Four Noble Truths deal directly with the problem of craving as an endless cycle of seeking pleasure and avoiding pain. Smokers, drinkers, or overeaters may think they are gaining great pleasure from indulging in their negative, unwholesome habit, but the pleasure is always transitory, leading to the pain of withdrawal, followed by another indulgence, and the pleasure/pain cycle continues. The real problem is not the specific one—cigarettes, alcohol, or caloric foods. It is more general—the endless battle between seeking pleasure and avoiding pain. This must be addressed on a deeper level to change.

Meditate to help you overcome your attraction to pleasure and aversion to pain. Learn detachment and experience emptiness. Then, where is your craving?

What Pleasures Do You Really Need?

So much of what we think we need we don't: The "nice to have" versus the "need to have." The number of things we need to have is small, but the number of things we might want to have is larger. Buddha encourages us to want less, to set aside craving for things to fill the void in our lives. You will discover true satisfaction that no want can possibly fulfill.

Meditation on Cravings and the Void

When you have a craving, like something is missing and you want to fill it, sit down to meditate. Stay with that feeling. Don't label it as something negative. Emptiness is a fertile void, full of potential. Try to tolerate and even embrace your feeling. Soon your craving may begin to alter so that it has less of a pull on you.

Working through Cravings

Question why you really need this habit so much. Perhaps you have defined yourself as this or that type of person who needs it, but remember that in your deeper, true nature, you were not born with this need. You developed it through your own thoughts and experiences. You can become detached from the craving, the need, through your own inner renunciation.

Follow the Eightfold Path. Go back to the earlier lessons and think through your unwanted habit. Get to know every detail of your craving with mindfulness meditations. Notice what you are doing as you do it. And meditate several times a day. Stay with it. This kind of personal work, when coupled with appropriate professional care, can help you to master your situation and yourself and find the tranquil wisdom of Nirvana.

Facing Discomfort Mindfully: You Can Stand It

We fear pain and discomfort. But paradoxically we perpetuate pain by trying to avoid it. Psychology has a theory that helps to explain why avoidance does not relieve suffering, called the Two-Process Theory of Avoidance (Domjan 1998, 259). First comes the original experience that brings about fear. Then comes avoidance of the feared situation. The problem with avoidance is that instead of relieving fear, it perpetuates it. One way to get over the troublesome behavior is to learn to face it. Exposure Therapy uses this method to help people get over various types of problems. People face the feared situation and go through it several times. By facing the problem, the emotional discomfort lessens.

We add to our pain, fear, and discomfort when we overreact and get overly emotional about it, taking it personally. We may feel our discomfort, and feel that we can't stand it—it's awful, terrible, and perhaps we add that our own, personal suffering is unique, far worse than that of others. Emotional concern is related to its closeness to us personally. The closer it is to us, the more we care. But this does not mean the world revolves around us.

We are not the center of the universe in this way. We are the center in a different way. We are One with the world, not different from it. The center is everywhere and nowhere to the known. So our caring about ourselves should not be so narrowly selective. And although life may seem uncomfortable and filled with misfortune, we can stand it if we have faith and trust in the unknown. Our thoughts about events that happen can add to or subtract from their personal emotional impact and meaning. But the events still are just what they are. Any interpretation is only one possible interpretation, from one perspective. As Nagarjuna would advise, change the belief system by letting go of believing absolutely in any system, not by just substituting another, alternative system. Change on a deeper level. A system itself is limiting.

Exercise for Facing Discomfort Mindfully
The avoidance cycle is created by the mind. But because it comes from the mind, you can work on it. Begin by trying to face discomfort.

When you forgo the extra dessert, drink, or cigarette, you may feel discomfort. Notice mindfully what you feel. Meditate on your sensations without evaluating them as good or bad. Just stay with your moment-to-moment experience. Face your discomfort and accept it for what it is. Clear your mind in meditation. Stay with each moment, without thought, without fear, without discomfort. Your experience is just what it is, an experience in this moment. Then discomfort diminishes, eventually leaving completely. You are empty and peaceful.

Substitute Wholesome Action
for Unwholesome Action

Sometimes people who get involved in cravings feel like their life is worthless and so why not indulge themselves in a harmful habit. But if you feel like your life is worthless, why not devote your life to helping someone else with no return, nothing to gain personally? By giving yourself, you discover the inner goodness that is within. Devotion to others can be a surprising source for self-cure. The famous psychologist Alfred Adler believed that caring about and helping others is central to mental health:

It is almost impossible to exaggerate the value of an increase in social feeling. The mind improves, for intelligence is a communal function. The feeling of worth and value is heightened, giving courage and an optimistic view. The individual feels at home in life and feels his existence to be worthwhile . . . All failures . . . are failures because they are lacking in social interest (Adler and Deutsch 1959, 42).

Substitute wholesome thoughts and actions for unwholesome ones. So whenever you feel like indulging in your negative habit, instead try lending a helping hand to someone else. Get involved in a benevolent project or volunteer work. You might find yourself craving the positive effects of compassionate action!

Remove the obstacles and you will discover enlightenment in your everyday life. Changes in your attunement and lifestyle can take time, so be patient with the process. Stay attuned and aware, meditate regularly, and don't be afraid to seek help if you need it. Enlightenment is always available if you are willing to clear the path and then walk it!

Living
Enlightenment

We weave the cloth
Of our every day
By what we do and give
The fabric of our destiny
Is made of how we live.
    —C. Alexander Simpkins

In ancient times, the perfect wisdom of Nirvana offered a clear and calm orientation to living, with compassion and caring for others. But people may wonder if such a lifestyle can really be translated into modern times. Can you incorporate a wise and compassionate lifestyle while still being fully engaged in the world today? The answer is yes. The Bodhisattva ideal is timeless. It adapts very naturally to our modern century. The basic human qualities of compassion and wisdom never go out of style. They keep improving. The challenge is greater than ever.

Lotus, Chang, Tai-ch'ien. 1958, Chinese. Ink and pigment. Gift of Ambassador and Mrs. Everett F. Drumright, San Diego Museum of Art.

When you are really aware and in tune, you will be more competent and engaged, not less.

Living as a Bodhisattva

You may start out seeking release from suffering and the tranquility of Nirvana. But as you train in meditation, you inevitably become immersed in a broader perspective: the interconnected, unified nature of the universe. Then you can re-engage in your life with renewed purpose, for the benefit of all. The highest ideal is not a solitary Nirvana for your own limited and separate ego. Instead, the rest of the world of beings must be included for your own complete happiness.

You Are Free to Choose

> Buddhism is concerned with the salvation of a human as a person who unlike other living beings has self-conscious and free will and thereby alone has the potential to become aware of and emancipated from the transience common to all things in the universe (Abe 1995, 212).

Anyone can be a bodhisattva, even people who are working at jobs, raising a family, or in school. The human capacity for mindfulness makes this possible. We are fortunate, because with this ability to be aware comes a calm, confident, happy life. When people are fully mindful, wisdom guides action, not impulse. Human potential develops to its fullest.

Taking Responsibility

Unfortunately, we often pass up many opportunities for fulfillment because we believe that we are incapable. We blame the outside world for preventing us from realizing our potential. But we have free will as long as we are willing to take responsibility.

Think of the word *responsibility* as two separate words: *response* and *ability*—the ability to respond. You have that ability if you are willing to take it. Sometimes taking responsibility is difficult when the choices are uncomfortable or the consequences are costly. It feels easier to blame someone else if the odds seem stacked up against you. But when you take responsibility, you gain far more than you risk.

Reclaiming Responsibility

Taking responsibility begins in your own mind. Turn your attention to your inner monologue that goes on through your day. Change statements such as "It makes me unhappy" to "I am unhappy about that." Or "So-and-so is bothering me" to "I am bothered by so and so." Notice that in the former statements you are making a decision to give up responsibility for what you feel and think. Although people or circumstances may try to persuade you, no one ultimately controls what you feel or think. You may not be able to change a situation, but you always have a choice as to how you respond.

Choosing an Enlightened Life

As you feel your own ability to make conscious decisions, you can choose the kind of life you want to live. You can decide to be a bodhisattva no matter what your circumstances of life may be. Rich or poor, young or old, the bodhisattva lifestyle can be your lifestyle.

Think carefully about your commitments. Knowing that you can choose your destiny, will you make a commitment to a wiser and more compassionate lifestyle? The choice is yours to make.

The Bodhisattva Nature

Bodhisattvas take vows to devote themselves to deepening their wisdom while also being compassionate. The lifestyle begins deliberately at first, but with careful training and persistence, eventually becomes natural and instinctive.

Bodhisattvas are the helpers of humanity, the people who make a difference in the world, who care about the needs of others. They are capable of patience, even when life pressures them. They develop the hardiness and perseverance to stay committed to their ideals. Work on integrating these traits into your own life, and the bodhisattva path opens up naturally.

Developing Your Bodhisattva Nature

Use your mindful awareness to help you develop bodhisattva qualities. For example, when you are feeling impatient with someone, notice what you feel. Then stop, relax your breathing, and meditate for a few moments. Remember the Path. Perhaps then you can be more understanding and give the other person the time they need.

Use your meditation to help you persevere and stay committed to helping. Begin with small challenges and keep mindful of the process. Working out a muscle makes it stronger. Similarly, exercising your bodhisattva qualities will make them grow and develop.

Compassionate Living

Compassion is a natural part of the human character. Psychologist Alfred Adler believed that compassion for others is an inherent trait in the healthy personality. He said, "Empathy and understanding are facts of social feeling, of harmony with the universe" (Adler and Deutsch 1959, 43).

Empathy is our tool for reaching out from our own being to others. Empathy involves a capacity to feel and understand another person from their perspective. Thus, empathy helps to express compassion in ways that matter. When you care about what other people are feeling and needing, an impulse to help them may naturally arise.

Empathy can have a powerfully positive effect and is an important quality for compassionate living. The famous psychologist Carl Rogers said, "Empathy is one of the most delicate and powerful ways we have of using ourselves" (Rogers 1980, 137).

Psychologists learn how to become more empathetic in order to help their clients. What is involved is an extension of mindfulness. You can take the awareness skills you have developed and direct your awareness to the world. By increasing your empathetic sensitivities you will be able to help others in ways that naturally reach beyond your own ego and truly touch and enhance another's world of meaning. These next exercises can help you to develop your skills with empathy.

Mindful Observation I

Using the skills from the mindfulness exercises in lesson 3, observe people in varied settings out in public. How are they dressed—the style, color of clothes. Notice details about their movements, ways of talking. Observe how they stand or sit. When walking, try listening to voice tones, footsteps, the rhythms and patterns of sound.

Mindful Observation II: Taking the Other Point of View

If can be a helpful word to evoke your empathy. Ask yourself, "If I were in that circumstance what would I think and feel?" Try to imagine yourself in the other person's situation. If you do, you can infer what the other might think or feel. Feel your own "as if" reaction, to understand what the other person could be feeling.

Initiating Compassionate Action

Compassion begins with your own Right Effort. Deliberately try to take a meaningful though simple compassionate action. Sometimes people think about doing some charitable volunteer work but decide that they don't have the time. But compassionate acts can also be small acts of kindness—even random ones—done in the course of a day. When paying for your items at a store, take the time to treat your salesperson or cashier with warmth and human kindness. Feed a wild bird in the park or help out at an animal shelter.

You can also extend compassion under stressful circumstances. Show other drivers courtesy on the roads, yielding, letting people pass if they get pressured. Don't lose your temper and honk your horn or yell if you feel impatient with traffic. Do your part to make the roads safe by considerate driving.

Be considerate and extend kindness in other situations as well. Be thoughtful of the people in your life when opportunities arise. Let your family and friends know that you care and are willing to help. Try to empathize, to understand what is actually needed as they would want it. Extend your empathetic caring to coworkers and further, to acquaintances. You may be pleasantly surprised as the ripples of your kindness spread out gently into the world.

Deepening the Spiritual Dimension

The Dalai Lama believes that there is a fundamental spiritual nature, common to all humanity. We have the potential for spirituality. And when we spontaneously express love, tolerance, forgiveness, kindness, and compassion, our natural spirituality is the source. Through the ages many great thinkers have embraced this idea. Mencius, the famous Confucian philosopher, believed that people have a built-in capacity to care. He pointed out that when a child is in trouble, most people will instinctively rush in to help. When people attune to their deeper, true nature, they will find a positive core.

Then how can you tap into your own spiritual potential? Train your mind, attitudes, and emotions: "True spirituality is a mental attitude that you can practice at any time" (Cutter and the Dalai Lama, 1998 299).

Turning the Tides

A wise Okinawan martial arts master taught his students that karate was to smile in any situation. The students left the class mystified. What did he mean?

On his way home one of the students came upon a group of American servicemen who were drunk and looking for a fight. They saw the student and started slinging derogatory insults at him. The annoyed student immediately felt like teaching them a lesson. Eager to use his fighting skills, he rolled up his sleeves to get ready. But just as he was about to attack, the sensei appeared.

The master confidently walked over to the servicemen with a warm smile and a friendly hand extended as he said, "Hello! Welcome to Okinawa!" He offered his hand to each of the surprised Americans, who couldn't help but shake his hand and return the smile. Within a few minutes they were all laughing and talking together. The sensei invited the servicemen out to dinner. They decided to do it and enjoyed a dinner together, which they wanted to pay for! They soon became friends, and when they learned that he taught martial arts, some wanted to study with him. Now the student understood the master's lesson.

Practice warmth and kindness wherever you are, in any situation. Stay attuned and in touch with the situation as it unfolds. Be mindful as you follow the stream of experiencing, moment by moment.

Some of the most useful learning can come when you are challenged. Hemingway defined courage as grace under pressure. It is easy to be happy and fearless when everything is going smoothly, but much more difficult when circumstances are trying.

So next time you face a tough situation such as when someone is angry with you, or if something bad has happened, try approaching it as a bodhisattva. First approach the situation with wisdom: be aware of what is happening, listen to what the person is saying, and consider the other point of view within a broader context of meaning that can encompass both perspectives, as one. Then pause, meditate for a few moments, and relax. Try to respond compassionately from a calm center. If you can address the problem without adding fuel to the fire, you alter the dynamics of the situation. Sometimes the other person's reaction is irrational. In such cases, by pausing rather than just reacting angrily, you may be able to offer the other person the space to act more maturely. Very often, you can meet life's challenges more effectively if you are aware, centered, and willing to be compassionate.

Everyday Life Is Enlightenment

Nirvana is Samsara. This means that enlightenment is to be found right in the midst of our daily existence. But how does the idea that Nirvana is Samsara actually translate into everyday life?

The answer to this question is in learning to live the ideal and real as One. Oneness spans the ideal and the real: Nirvana and Samsara together. Everyday life gives many opportunities to live in this ideal way, to be the ideal, not as ideal in a manner apart from this world, but as a real and active part of it. This paradox between real and ideal is resolved by living.

Since ultimately, on the absolute level, we are all One, part of the universal Buddha nature, caring about others is actually caring about ourselves as well. Therefore, we must take others seriously. This ultimate ideal of universal compassion is a big job, but it can be approached in small ways, not just as all or nothing. We partake of the bodhisattva spirit in a small way when we do a positive thing for others without thought or concern for ourselves. When we help others feel less suffering, less distress from the inevitable negatives of life, the tragic losses and frustrations, for a moment we are bodhisattvas. And in those moments, ideal and real are one: Nirvana is Samsara.

Nirvana is Samsara translates as peacefulness of mind, freed from selfish desires or petty concerns. This wise and compassionate adjustment is not easily lost with mind clear and focused on life. Accepting the Way, everyday problems no longer distract from the Path; they are part of it:

> Enlightenment is enlightenment because it enlightens all
> our motives, desires, whims, determinations, impulses,
> thoughts, etc. . . . In an enlightened mind, a feeling or

thought as it occurs is purified and freed from the taints of ignorance and egoism (Shaku 1987, 139).

So let go of a narrow, ego-centered point of view and see through the eyes of a wider, enlightened vision. With every moment, every experience of interaction, you can choose to respond with compassion and caring. And not just because of fear of consequences or obedience to a moral imperative, but because you hear the rhythm of the universal and are in tune with its harmony.

The system of relationships is connected, such that each individual part is intimately part of the whole, the unity. So any one part of the system meaningfully reflects others. In a practical sense, then, we do not just prepare and prepare until we get to another place called Nirvana. Instead, living out our lives now is a reflection of Nirvana, the thread of the fabric. So cherish the peak moments, which can be little mini-enlightenments while continuing to be mindful of the details of your everyday life.

Meditation is the tool to help you understand the true nature of Nirvana in everyday life. This understanding evolves as you experience how meditation is more than a method. When practiced well, you as the meditator are no longer separate from the act of meditating. Immersed in the moment, you and the world become One. When you can feel Oneness in yourself, your Samsara truly is Nirvana.

In Tibetan Buddhism, the bodhisattva keeps coming back. After all, if you are fully committed to helping others to relieve their suffering, then to continue to return is positive, flowing with the intent. You can keep coming back to the ideal, expressing it in the real world. Then the real and the ideal will become One.

Far away in time and space
The moon glows clear
Meditation's peaceful calm,
Brings far to near
Distance dissolves in the mind
Wisdom is here.
—C. Alexander Simpkins

Bibliography

Abe, Masao. 1995. *Buddhism and Interfaith Dialogue*. Honolulu: University of Hawaii Press.

———. 1985. *Zen and Western Thought*. Honolulu: University of Hawaii Press.

Adler, Kurt A. and Danica Deutsch, eds. 1959. *Essays in Individual Psychology: Contemporary Application of Alfred Adler's Theories*. New York: Grove Press, Inc.

Baudouin, Charles. 1921. *Suggestion and Autosuggestion*. New York: Ballantine Books.

Berkeley, George. 1820. *The Works of George Berkeley*. London: Richard Priestley.

Bruno, Richard Louis. 1999. Buddhism Plus Disability. *New Mobility* www.newmobility.com.

Cheng, Hsueh-li. 1982. *Nagarjuna's Twelve Gate Treatise*. Dordrecht, Holland: D. Reidel Publishing Company.

Collingwood, R.G. 1957. *The Idea of History*. New York: Oxford University Press.

Conze, Edward. 1951. *Buddhism: Its Essence and Development*. New York: Philosophical Library.

————. 1995. *A Short History of Buddhism*. Oxford, England: Oneworld Publications.

Cutter, Howard C. and His Holiness The Dalai Lama. 1998. *The Art of Happiness*. New York: Riverhead Books.

Domjan, Michael. 1998. *The Principles of Learning and Behavior*. Pacific Grove, Calif.: Brooks/Cole Publishing Company.

Dumoulin, Heinrich. 1988. *Zen Buddhism: A History*. New York: Macmillan Publishing Company.

Fisher, Mary Pat. 1994. *Living Religions*. Englewood Cliffs, N.J.: Prentice Hall.

Frank, Jerome D. and Julia B. Frank. 1991. *Persuasion and Healing*. Baltimore, Md.: Johns Hopkins University Press.

Gyatso, Tenzin. 1994. *The World of Tibetan Buddhism*. Boston: Wisdom Publications.

Haugh, Sheila and Tony Merry. 2001. *Empathy*. Ross-on-Wye, England: PCCS Books.

Hanh, Thich Nhat. 1998. *The Heart of the Buddha's Teaching*. Berkeley, Calif.: Parallax Press.

————. 1992. *The Diamond That Cuts Through Illusion*. Berkeley, Calif.: Parallax Press.

Hothersall, David. 1995. *History of Psychology*. New York: McGraw-Hill, Inc.

Huntington, C.W. Jr. 1989. *The Emptiness of Emptiness*. Honolulu: University of Hawaii Press.

James, William. 1896. *The Principles of Psychology*. 2 vols. New York: Macmillan.

Buddhism in Ten

Kerouac, Jack. 1960. *The Scripture of the Golden Eternity*. San Francisco: New City Lights Books, 1994.

Levine, Marvin. 2000. *The Positive Psychology of Buddhism and Yoga*. Mahwah, N.J.: Lawrence Erlbaum Associates, Publishers.

Locke, John. 1975. *An Essay Concerning Human Understanding*. Oxford, England: Clarendon Press.

Mizuno, Koben. 1995. *Buddhist Sutras: Origin, Development, Transmission*. Tokyo: Kosei Publishing Co.

Moore, Charles A. Ed. 1968. *The Japanese Mind: Essentials of Japanese Philosophy and Culture*. Honolulu: University of Hawaii Press.

Perls, Frederick S. 1969. *Gestalt Therapy Verbatim*. Lafayette, Calif.: Real People Press.

Price, A. F. and Wong Mou-lam. 1990. *The Diamond Sutra & The Sutra of Hui-Neng*. Boston: Shambhala.

Radhakrishnan, Sarvepalli. 1977. *Indian Philosophy*, Vol. 1. London: George Allen & Unwin Ltd.

Rogers, Carl. 1980. *A Way of Being*. Boston: Houghton Mifflin Co.

Sartre, Jean-Paul. 1965. *Essays in Existentialism*. Secaucus, N.J.: Citadel Press.

Shaku, Soyen. 1987. *Zen for Americans*. New York: Dorset Press.

Simpkins, C. Alexander and Annellen M. 2000. *Simple Buddhism: A Guide to Enlightened Living*. Boston: Tuttle Publishing.

———. 2003. *Zen in Ten: Easy Lessons for Spiritual Growth*. Boston: Tuttle Publishing.

———. 2002. *Tao In Ten: Easy Lessons for Spiritual Growth*. Boston: Tuttle Publishing.

———. 2001. *Timeless Teachings from the Therapy Masters*. San Diego, Calif.: Radiant Dolphin Press.

————. 2001. *Simple Tibetan Buddhism: A Guide to Tantric Living*. Boston: Tuttle Publishing.

————. 1999. Simple Zen: *A Guide to Living Moment by Moment*. Boston: Tuttle Publishing.

————. 1999. *Simple Taoism: A Guide to Living in Balance*. Boston: Tuttle Publishing.

————. 1997. *Zen around the World: A 2500-Year Journey from the Buddha to You*. Boston: Tuttle Publishing.

Smith, Houston. 1991. *The World's Religions*. San Francisco: Harper San Francisco.

Spiegelberg, Frederic. 1961. *Zen, Rocks, and Waters*. New York: Pantheon Books.

Spiller, R. E. ed. 1965. *Selected Essays, Lectures, and Poems of Ralph Waldo Emerson*. New York: Pocket Books.

Stevens, John O. ed. 1975. *Gestalt Is*. Moab, Utah: Real People Press.

Suzuki, Daisetz Teitaro. 1994. *The Training of the Zen Buddhist Monk*. Boston: Charles E. Tuttle Co., Inc.

The Tate Gallery. 1980. *Towards a New Art: Essays on the Background to Abstract Art 1910–1920*. London: The Tate Gallery Publications Department.

Westgeest, Helen. 1997. *Zen in the Fifties*. Amsterdam, The Netherlands. Waanders Publishers, Zwolle.

Yanagi, Soetsu. 1981. *The Unknown Craftsman*. Tokyo: Kodansha International Ltd.

Yokoi, Yuho. 1990. *Zen Master Dogen*. New York: Weatherhill.

Yutang, Lin. 1942. *The Wisdom of China and India*. New York: Random House, 1955.